What the Mystics Know

RICHARD ROHR

WHAT THE
MYSTICS
KNOW

Seven Pathways to Your Deeper Self

☩

A CROSSROAD BOOK
The Crossroad Publishing Company
New York

The Crossroad Publishing Company

www.crossroadpublishing.com
© 2015 by The Crossroad Publishing Company, Inc.

First paperback edition printed 2019

Library of Congress Cataloging-in-Publication Data available from the Library of Congress.

ISBN: 978-0-8245-9965-2 (paperback)
ISBN: 978-0-8245-2039-7 (cloth)

Cover design by: George Foster
Book design by: Eve Vaterlaus

Books published by The Crossroad Publishing Company may be purchased at special quantity discount rates for classes and institutional use.
For information, please email info@crossroadpublishing.com.

Printed in the United States of America

CONTENTS

INTRODUCTION

I HOPE THAT THIS BOOK CAN INVITE you into the seemingly simple yet always profound realm of those who have found their way close to God and all of creation, and it can place the path of the mystic within your reach. We have failed our people profoundly by mystifying the very notion of mysticism.

Can seeing with the eyes of mystics really have relevance in our busy modern world? I think it is not only relevant but absolutely necessary to change our levels of consciousness, which many religious traditions might have also called growth in holiness or divine union. As Einstein said, but now in my own words, we have tried to solve today's problems with yesterday's software—which often caused the problem in the first place. Through a regular practice of contemplation we can awaken to the profound presence of the unitive Spirit, which then gives us the courage and capacity to face the paradox that everything is—ourselves included. Higher levels of consciousness always allow us to include and understand more. Deeper levels of divine union allow us to forgive and show compassion toward more and more, even those we are not naturally attracted to, or even our enemies.

Mystics have plumbed the depths of both suffering and love and emerged with depths of compassion for the world, and a learned capacity to recognize God within themselves, in others, and in all things. If we can read with an attitude of simple mindfulness, the insights and practices shared here can equip us with a deep and embracing peace, even in the presence of the many kinds of limitation and suffering that life offers us. From such contact with the deep rivers of grace, we can live our lives from a place of nonjudgment, forgiveness, love, and a quiet contentment with the ordinariness of our lives. Knowing now that it is not ordinary at all!

Through each of the seven pathways outlined in the book, we can discover, in the context of a mature Christianity, or any religion, the God who is "closer to me than I am to myself," as St. Augustine puts it. Through the use of scriptures and both traditional and new metaphors, I want to give thoughtful guidance from classic sources, so you can know that your experience is not just your experience but the common domain of the perennial, or wisdom, traditions, which will always come to the surface in every age. How else can we distinguish the guidance of the Holy Spirit from our own egoic whims and fantasies?

Read a small passage from this book—all selected by others from a lifetime of speaking and writing—and carry it with you in your thoughts, hearts, and prayers throughout the day, and then notice what rises up within you. By applying what the mystics know to your momentary outlook, you will be able to bring openheartedness into the life you lead and the work you do. Then you might just be able to recognize that the ordinary path can also be the way of the mystic. It is all a matter of the eyes and the heart.

I want to full-heartedly dedicate this book to the love, work, and memory of a dear friend, John Jones. He was more excited about making this book happen than I was! He used his own time, with the full support of Gwendolin Herder and Cross-road Press to make this book happen. John was able to see and deeply value things that I had said as I merely grasped for words that might express my own inner experience—things I often wrote only intuitively or haphazardly. It was he who had the wisdom and perception of the saints to know what I really wanted to say!

John Jones had the courage and clarity to perceive the seven underlying themes that became this small book. When the Crossroad staff quietly presented the first draft to me, after John had tragically passed over—so young—I could only sigh and weep, and recognize that he was still my friend, but now from the other side. I thank you, John, a truly good man! For that is what you are.

Part One

THE ENLIGHTENMENT YOU SEEK ALREADY DWELLS WITHIN YOU

We don't think ourselves into a new way of living.
We live ourselves into a new way of thinking.

HOW DO WE FIND WHAT IS ALREADY THERE?

How do you find what is supposedly already there? Why isn't it obvious? How do you awaken the Center? By thinking about it? By praying and meditating? By more silence and solitude? Yes, perhaps, but mostly by living—and living consciously. The edges suffered and enjoyed lead us back to the Center. The street person feels cold and rejection and has to go to a deeper place for warmth. The hero pushes against his own self-interested edges and finds that they don't matter. The alcoholic woman recognizes how she has hurt her family and breaks through to a compassion beyond her. In each case, the edges suffer, inform, partially self-destruct, and all are found to be unnecessary and even part of the problem. That which feels the pain also lets it go, and the Center stands revealed and sufficient! We do not find our own Center; it finds us. The body is in the soul. It is both the place of contact and the place of surrender.

We don't think ourselves into a new way of living. We live ourselves into a new way of thinking. The journeys around the circumference lead us to life at the Center. Then by what is certainly a vicious and virtuous circle, the Center calls all the journeys at the circumference into question! The ruthless ambition of the businessman can lead him to the very failure and emptiness that is the point of his conversion. Is the ambition therefore good or evil? Do we really have to sin to know salvation? Call me a "sin mystic," but that is exactly what I see happening in all my pastoral experience.

That does not mean that we should set out intentionally to sin. We only see the pattern after the fact. Julian of Norwich put it perfectly: "Commonly, first we fall and later we see it and both are the Mercy of God." How did we ever lose that? It got hidden away in that least celebrated but central Easter Vigil service, when the deacon sings to the church about a felix culpa, the happy fault that precedes and necessitates the eternal Christ. Like all great mysteries of faith, it is hidden except to those who keep vigil and listen.

A TRUE MIRROR

From my first days as a Franciscan, we were told that we were "Christian humanists." I glory in being a humanist. I have no problem seeing the goodness in people as a true mirror of the goodness in God. For me, there is a direct correlation. . . .

We are reflections of the invisible God *(Gen. 1:27)*. And our only way to know God is through this humanity. This is our only road to a little enlightenment. . . . We begin here. If I'm created in the image and likeness of God, then anthropology might be just as important as theology to understand the mystery of God. . . .

We must never think we are building up God by putting humanity down. We would, instead, be insulting God, blaspheming, to set ourselves against God's creation.

TO BUILD YOUR OWN HOUSE

To pray is to build your own house. To pray is to discover that Someone else is within your house. To pray is to recognize that it is not your house at all. To keep praying is to have no house to protect because there is only One House. And that One House is everybody's Home. In other words, those who pray from the heart actually live in a very different and ultimately dangerous world. It is a world that makes the merely physical world seem anemic, illusory, and relative. The

word "real" takes on a new meaning, and we find ourselves judging with utterly new scales, weights, and standards. Be careful of such house-builders, for their loyalties will lie in very different directions. They will be very different kinds of citizens, and the state will not so easily depend on their salute. That is the politics of prayer. And that is probably why truly spiritual people are always a threat to politicians of any sort. They want our allegiance, and we can no longer give it, our house is too big.

LIKE A MUSTARD SEED

> Then Jesus asked, "What is the kingdom of God like?
> What shall I compare it to? It is like a mustard seed,
> which a man took and planted in his garden. It grew and
> became a tree, and the birds perched in its branches.
>
> *(Luke 13:18–19)*

This parable is instructive for people who want the kingdom to happen right now—they want to be holy after their first year on the journey. For the kingdom to happen, however, we have to walk the entire journey. The kingdom of heaven is like a mustard seed. It starts small, but it keeps growing. So

keep growing. As time goes on, you'll sprout many branches, and you'll look out at the end of your life and say, "God has done it. God has been faithful to the promise. God has made beauty out of my little life."

DYNAMIS, OUR TRUE SELF

A biblical definition of the Holy Spirit is *dynamis*, which means "power" or "strength." We are talking about the power that gives us the certainty that God is drawing us near and that we are associated with the Holy.

... If we "work our way through" our compulsion and emerge again on the other side, then we stand before the depths of our self. There we find a purified passion, a chastened power, our best and true self. Tradition has called this place the "soul," the point where the human being and God meet, where unity is possible, and where religion consists not only of words, norms, dogmas, rituals, and visits to church, but becomes a genuine experience of encounter.

DISCOVERING SELF-WORTH

Self-worth is not created; it is discovered.

SEARCHING FOR WHAT WE HAVE ALREADY TOUCHED

You can only miss something that you have searched for and partially experienced. In fact, you do not even search for it until you have already touched it.

WHEN FAITH CREATES WHAT IT DESIRES

Faith is not a means to something further. It is not what we do in order to get into heaven. Mutual perfect faith would be heaven! Faith is its own end. To have faith is already to have come alive. "Your faith has saved you" is the way Jesus put it to the blind man *(Luke 18:42).*

Faith is the opposite of resentment, cynicism, and negativity. Faith is always, finally, a self-fulfilling prophecy. Faith actually begins to create what it desires. Faith always recreates the good world. Without faith, you sink into the bad world that you most feared. With faith, you keep trusting, hoping, believing, and calling forth life from stones, which is exactly what Jesus intimates in the chapter that follows his healing of the blind man *(Luke 19:40).* You can call life forth from anything if you already possess life. You can make a stone breathe, make it live for you, make it shout out in praise of God. As has been so often said, faith is a matter of having new eyes, seeing everything through and even with the eyes of God.

WE ARE ALREADY HOLY

"How can I be more holy?" We don't have to make ourselves holy. We already are, and we just don't know it. In Christian terminology it is called the Divine Indwelling or the free gift of the Holy Spirit. That proclamation, and all that proceeds from it, is the essential, foundational, and primary task of all religion. Thus, authentic religion is more about subtraction than addition, more letting go of the false self than any attempt at engineering a true self. You can't create what you already have.

RADICAL RESPONSIBILITY

How can we really be liberated? How can we pass on this freedom to the world? I would like to clarify this question on the basis of a story *(from Luke 8)* about a miraculous cure.

Then they arrived at the country of the Gerasenes, which is opposite Galilee. And as Jesus stepped out on land, there met him a man from the city who had demons; for a long time he had worn no clothes, and he lived not in a house but among the tombs.

This is a picture of a man who lives among the dead and isn't quite civilized, because he runs around naked. We shall soon see that the city is comfortable with the fact that this man lives out there, and so is he. Because when Jesus comes to him, we are told:

When he saw Jesus, he cried out and fell down before him, and said in a loud voice: "What have you to do with me, Jesus, Son of the Most High God? I beseech you, do not torment me." The man did not know whether he wanted what Jesus had. His unfreedom was the only world he knew.

We feel much more comfortable with our slavery than with freedom. Freedom means that we have to assume radical responsibility for what we are. To be enslaved means that we always have somebody else to blame for our problems. An evil spirit had already possessed this man for a long time: "He was bound with chains and fetters." In this way people tried to keep him under control. Although they kept him chained, they said the evil spirit was holding him captive. When we project the darkness in us onto another person or other groups, then these people or groups end up accepting our projection. Sooner or later we all believe the world's version of who we are.

TELLING OUR OWN STORY

Why does a story have such power? Because most of us don't think abstractly. We live in a world of images and symbols; that's what moves us. . . . Each of us is a story. We were created by God as a story waiting to be told, and each of us has to find a way to tell our story. In the telling of it we come to recognize and own ourselves. People without a place to tell their story and a person to listen to it never come into possession of themselves. . . . For many people, "myth" means something that isn't true. Please put aside that understanding. Myth is, in fact, something that is so true that it can be adequately expressed only in story, symbol, and ritual. It can't be abstracted and objectified. Its meaning and mystery are so deep and broad that they can be presented only in story form. When you step into a story, you find it is without limits and you can walk around with it and inside it. It is natural to sing, dance, and reenact a story. It is too big and too deep to be merely "understood" or taught.

AWAKING FROM OUR SLEEP

We long for distant absolutes, perhaps seeking a confirmation of the absolute we already intuit within ourselves. Like Jacob we eventually awake from our sleep and say, "God was in this place, and I never knew it!" *(Gen. 28:16)*.

JULIAN OF NORWICH AND THE FIRST NUMINOUS EXPERIENCE

There is the first numinous experience that opens our eyes. It only needs to happen once. It happened to Julian of Norwich, the English mystic, one May 8, and she lived off of it for the rest of her life. She tried to describe it in her writings, which she called "Showings." That night, God showed her his heart. Nothing more happened. People such as Angela Merici, who founded the Ursulines, and Junipero Serra had religious experiences at seventeen and eighteen that told them

what they were going to do, and neither of them did it until they were fifty-five.

From eighteen to fifty-five was the unfolding. Then, when it happened at fifty-five, they knew what they were born for. When that moment comes, it is great and it is all synchronicity. We know then that grace is at work and we are not manufacturing our own lives.

GOD IS CHOOSING US NOW

My starting point is that we're already there. We cannot attain the presence of God because we're already totally in the presence of God. What's absent is awareness. Little do we realize that God is maintaining us in existence with every breath we take. As we take another it means that God is choosing us now and now and now. We have nothing to attain or even learn. We do, however, need to unlearn some things.

To become aware of God's presence in our lives, we have to accept what is often difficult, particularly for people in what appears to be a successful culture. We have to accept that human culture is in a mass hypnotic trance. We're sleepwalkers. All religious teachers have recognized that we human beings do not naturally see; we have to be taught how to see. That's what religion is for. That's why the Buddha and Jesus say with one voice, "Be awake." Jesus talks about "staying watchful" *(Matt. 25:13; Luke 12:37; Mark 13:33–37)*, and "Buddha" means "I am awake" in Sanskrit. Jesus says further, "If your eye is healthy, your whole body is full of light" *(Luke 11:34)*.

Thus, we have to learn to see what is there. Such a simple directive is hard for us to understand. We want to attain some concrete information or achieve an improved morality or learn some behavior that will make us into superior beings. Bu there's no question here of meritocracy. Although we have a "merit badge" mentality, prayer shows us that we are actually "punished" by any expectation of merit and reward. For that expectation keeps us from the truly transformative experience called grace. . . .

Experiencing radical grace is like living in another world. It's not a world in which I labor to get God to notice me and like me. It's not a world in which I strive for spiritual success. It's not a cosmic game of crime and punishment.

Unfortunately, a large percentage of the world's religions do teach that, if usually indirectly. Religious people are afraid of gratuity. Instead, we want God for the sake of social order, and we want religion for the sake of social controls.

I'd like to say something a bit different about prayer, and therefore about religion. Prayer is not primarily saying words or thinking thoughts. It is, rather, a stance. It's a way of living in the Presence, living in awareness of the Presence, and even of enjoying the Presence. The full contemplative is not just aware of the Presence, but trusts, allows, and delights in it.

PRESENCE AND NONDUALITY

This brilliant word, nonduality (*advaita* in Sanskrit), was used by many in different traditions in the East to distinguish from total and perfect absorption or enmeshment. Facing some of the same challenges of modern-day ecology and quantum physics, they did not want to say that all things were metaphysically or physically identical, nor did they want to separate and disconnect everything. In effect, the contemplative mind in East or West withholds from labeling things or categorizing them too quickly, so it can come to see them in themselves, apart from the words or concepts that become their substitutes.

Humans tend to think that because they agree or disagree with the idea of a thing, they have realistically encountered the thing itself. Not at all true, says the contemplative. It is necessary to encounter the thing in itself. "Presence" is my word for this encounter, a different way of knowing and touching the moment. It is much more vulnerable and leaves us without a sense of control. Such panoramic and deeper seeing requires a lot of practice, but the rewards are superb and, I believe, necessary for both joy and truth in this world.

Part Two
GOD IS FOUND IN IMPERFECTION

WHY THE JOURNEY MATTERS

Suppose a superstar of knowledge moves into your house as a boarder. With three Ph.D.s after his name, he sits at your supper table each evening dispensing information about nuclear physics, cyberspace, and psychoneuroimmunology, giving ultimate answers to every question you ask. He doesn't lead you through his thinking process, however, or even involve you in it; he simply states the conclusions he has reached.

You might find his conclusions interesting and even very helpful, but the way he relates to you will not set you free, empower you, or make you feel good about yourself. His wisdom will not liberate you, it will not invite you to growth and life—indeed, it will in the end make you feel inferior and dependent. That's exactly the way we have used Jesus. We have treated him like a person with three Ph.D.s coming to tell us his conclusions.

We humans don't really want conclusions. We want to experience the process. We want someone to walk with us through all the stages of faith; we want someone to hold our hand, to love us, to support us, and to believe in us while we are in process. You and I are always in process; that's where we live our lives; that's what interests us. Even our faith is in process. The fact is we're really not all that concerned about having perfect conclusions. We need someone to help us make sense of the journey itself.

THE WHEAT AND THE WEEDS

When the new wheat sprouted and then ripened,
the darnel [weeds] appeared as well.
The owner's servants went to him and said,
"Sir, was it not good seed that you sowed in your
field? If so, where does the darnel come from?"

(Matt. 13:26–27)

And that is always our question. Where do the weeds come from? We try to be good. We think we're Christian. Yet we have the most horrible thoughts. And we do things we do not understand. We hurt the very people we do not want to hurt. We know our own individual lives have brought their share of evil into this world. We feel guilty about that and we're sorry.

. . . In this parable we see that Jesus understands our struggle and inconsistency. "Some enemy has done this," the owner answered. Immediately we want to blame it on someone else. So the servants asked, "Do you want us to go and weed it out?" And Jesus gives a most extraordinary answer, a very different one from what most moralists and confessors have given us. Jesus says, "No, because when you weed out the weeds you might pull up the wheat with it. . . . Let them both grow until the harvest" *(Matt. 13:29–30)*. In the harvest, "I'll say to the reapers, 'Separate the weeds and the wheat.'" We are unwilling, it seems, to leave any work for the reapers.

We have spent most of our lives trying to do the job of separation ourselves, trying to figure out who the good guys are and who the bad guys are. It's a waste of time, Jesus seems to say.

USING EVIL FOR GOOD

The key moral question is not, "How can we get rid of evil?" but rather, "How can we use evil for good?" How can we learn discernment so that we can say, yes, this is weed and that is wheat, but they must both grow together to create life? That is the great moral question. That is the true challenge for spiritual guides—how to put together darkness and light.

GOD IS AN EARTHQUAKE

A Jewish master once said, "God is not nice. God is not an uncle. God is an earthquake." We've created a "bourgeois" version of Christianity that has manufactured a nice God. We want Jesus finally to take away our insecurity. We want to feel as if we are just wheat and not weeds. But God isn't nice, and God isn't an uncle. God is an earthquake. In a way the preaching of the Gospel pulls the rug out from under us. We have to put our life on a new footing. I believe we've always thought that we could reason our way into the Gospel. But we'll never solve the way to a new life in our heads; we have to live our way into a new kind of thinking. First we have to act.

SPIRITUALLY STARVING
IN THE MIDST OF PLENTY

A wall-eyed pike is put into an aquarium. He is fed for some days with little minnows. Then, in the middle of the experiment, a glass partition is placed down the middle of the aquarium so that the pike is now confined to one side.

Then the researchers drop the minnows on the other side. Immediately, the pike goes for the minnows, but he hits himself against the glass. He circles and hits it again. He tries a third time, but he is now hitting the glass a little less hard. After a few more times, he's just sort of nosing up against the glass. He has a feeling he's not going to get those minnows. Pretty soon, he just swims around in circles and ignores the minnows on the other side.

At that point, those doing the experiment take out the glass. The minnows come right up against the gills of the pike and he doesn't even try to eat them.

The experiment ends when the wall-eyed pike starves to death. He's convinced he's not going to get those minnows, so there's no point in wasting his time or hurting his nose again. That is the best image of cultural blindness I have heard. I wanted to weep when I first heard it, but I realized that the experiment is about human beings, not about fish. That's much of the human story, people spiritually starving in the midst of plenty. They don't know how to eat.

MAN GUARDS HIS NOTHING

Less than a block from my house in downtown Albuquerque, there is a sidewalk where the homeless often sit against the wall to catch the morning sun. A few days ago, I saw new graffiti chalked clearly on the pavement. It touched me so profoundly that I immediately went home and wrote it in my journal. It said, "I watch how foolishly man guards his nothing, thereby keeping us out. Truly God is hated here." I can only guess at what kind of person wrote such wisdom, but I heard a paraphrase of Jesus in mind: "The people of the sidewalk might well be at the Center, and the people in their houses might well be on the circumference" *(Luke 13:30; Mark 10:31; Matt. 19:30; 20:16)*. Now I can probably assume that this street person is not formally educated in theology or trained in contemplative spirituality. Yet from the edges, this person has clearly understood all that I am trying to say. Did she go through healing? Did he pay for psychotherapy? How does this person so clearly recognize the false nature of our self-image and yet the clear sense of being included and excluded? This street person has both edges and essence and also knows exactly who God is!

I AM PART OF THE PROBLEM

As we face our own inner Herods and Hitlers, we both recognize their disguises in others and we learn a certain forgiveness that is necessary for ongoing political involvement. I am always a part of the problem. I can never really stand apart, above, or beyond human sinfulness. I am a part of the tragic sense of life, and there is no perfect orthodoxy on which to stand.

THE COSMIC EGG

Today there seems to be a breach in almost every wall. Some have said, the "cosmic egg" that seemed to hold us together for a long time is now broken: "All the king's horses and all the king's men" find themselves unable to put it back together again. It feels as if the earth moved beneath us somewhere in the mid or late sixties: the old certitudes, the agreed-upon assumptions, the core values of Western civilization came up for major questioning. Our presuppositions dissolved, and the questioning has not stopped for decades. We now find ourselves engaged in major and sometimes minor culture wars on almost every personal and social issue.

It is all thinkable now, and most of us are beyond being shocked by anything. We are often sad, discouraged, and even alienated from the only world we have. It was so much easier to live inside the cosmic egg! It feels like exile from home, and it manifests in rampant abuse, violence, victim behavior, denial, social hysteria, or lifeboat ethics. Each enclave of security seems to be clutching at its small certitudes: defiant, assertive, and substituting opinions for deeper identity.

We yearn for breach-menders who can restore our ruined houses, as Isaiah says. We long for great-souled people who can hold the chaos together within themselves—and give us

the courage to do the same. In mythology this is the gift of the queen or the king. In religion it is symbolized by the temple in Jerusalem or the cathedral at the center of the city. In the psychological world, we speak simply of mental and emotional health. In spirituality, we dare to long for God. But our condition instead is always one of exile. We are "pilgrims and strangers on this earth" *(Heb. 11:13)*.

PRINCIPLES AND PRAYER

Law will always dominate people who have not experienced that the Spirit blows where it pleases *(John 3:8)* and cannot be controlled by our righteousness. Law is the false promise for those who control life from their heads, those who are afraid to listen anew right now, those who substitute principles for prayer and people. As St. Thomas More said, there is no better place to hide than "behind the thickets of the law." And he was a lawyer!

THE DEPTHS OF OUR EMPTINESS

Victory over sin is never total but rather a victory over sin's power to overwhelm us or defeat us. The sacred signs [in the form of stories, images, symbols, or dreams] allow us to live with and walk with and through our sin to God. God's help does not readjust our false self or polish up our self-image. Instead, God shows us the depths of our emptiness and sin so that we have nothing more to shock or humiliate us.

LIVING IN A BROKEN WORLD

Liberalism creates suspicious people more than loving people. Political liberals begin by asking, "Who has the power here?" instead of, "How can I serve here?" Life is an issue to be informed about or fixed, but seldom a mystery to participate in—even in its broken state. That is probably the core difference between a mere liberal and a truly transformed individual.

Liberals need to find that rare ability to live happily in a broken world and still work for its reform. It is a work of art that I believe only spirituality can achieve. Mere ideology is not sufficient to the task. Behind every cynic I meet, there was once a youthful idealist who could not make his ideas work outside of his head. Liberals seem incapable of being a part of a tainted anything: food, institutions, histories, explanations, groups, churches, and most especially authority structures of any kind. Soon they themselves cannot lead—or follow good leaders, because they mistrust power and leadership itself. Yet history makes it clear that good leadership is necessary for real change.

American liberalism, in my opinion, has no practical goal beyond maintaining personal and social freedom. "I choose, therefore I am" might be its operational belief system. The problem for a peace movement is that you cannot build any new social structures or enduring constituencies within this belief system. Such movements deconstruct from within, as the highly opinionated individualists quickly come into conflict with one another's freedom to think. What they lack is a spiritual center, a Reference Point outside of the private "I."

We religious folks would say they lack God, especially a God who gives source, pattern, and external goal. As a result, we each become our own source, pattern, and goal. The First Commandment was not accidentally the first, because if you don't have "one God before you," you will always become your own god. For this reason it is difficult to build anything cohesive or compelling among liberal people. There is no authority beyond individual opinion and recent research, and in fact, the very word "authority" is considered bad. Compare that to the true "liberalism" of a Martin Luther King, or a Dorothy Day, or a Cesar Chavez. They all had an authority beyond their own—and a Center outside of themselves.

ALL NEW PEOPLE

Our people are dying for lack of vision, for lack of transcendent meaning to name their soul and their struggles. What good is inclusive language if no one is even listening to our message? Why would a young person join a group of fifty-year-old complainers who are unwilling to speak of God and joy and peace beyond comprehension? These are the obsessive preoccupations of my generation who have had more freedom, change, our-way-of-arranging-the-world, than any generation in human history. Why are we unwilling to join in the cosmic dance that invites and thrills the would-be searchers? Why are so many of us, deconstructed more than we are aware, afraid to kneel and adore what is— in the only lifetime we will ever have? Don't we know, in the words of Anne Lamott, that a hundred years from now it will be "all new people"? We must give them something good to build on.

WE ARE THE MASKS OF GOD

The word "person" comes from the Latin word for "mask" or for the actor's "part" in a drama. The Judeo-Christian tradition would see all human personhood as a real and organic participation in the one personhood that is God. In other words, the human self has no meaning or substance apart from the Selfhood of God. God's personhood is not a mask, but the face behind all masks. We are the masks of God, and we play out God's image in myriad human ways. The immense problem we are facing in a secular society is that we do not know we are the masks of God. We are therefore condemned to creating our own significance, our own legitimation, our own mask and personhood. This makes us—like atoms—inherently unstable. When we do not see our lives as a participation in Another, we are forced to manufacture our own private significance. Contemporary psychology had to create a word for this, and again chose the Latin word for "I," or "ego." It is the atomized self, the small self, the false self, which does not really "exist" at all. In such a state of insecurity, it overdefends itself and overdefines itself. We call this the imperial ego, and it is the basis for all illusion and

all evil. It is Adam and Eve trying to survive outside of the Garden, and they can't.

REVEALING OUR NEEDINESS

Saint Francis of Assisi and the Buddha wanted their followers to be "mendicants." Begging seemed to create an ambience of respectful connection, vulnerability, and utter honesty: We are in this human thing together. We do not need to be afraid of one another, but we do need to reveal our "nakedness" and neediness to one another.

That was my first lesson in the ancient culture of India: there appeared to be a much finer line between ego and shadow. Ego and shadow were not as separate and defended, but somehow seemed to be working up front and together. When ego and shadow are a little kinder to one another, it is a humble spirit that is released.

SIN IS SOMETHING WE ARE

Sin is not simply something we do—it is something we are. Sin is the distorted personalities people are trapped in. Sin is the illusionary lives that people live and the twisted motives that drive them. No one has ever taught them truth or meaning, so they live at a very low spiritual subsistence level. They are "paralyzed" *(Luke 5)*. . . . Isolated actions or omissions are much more the effects of sin rather than sin itself.

WORTHY AND UNWORTHY

As Dorothy Day once wisely said, "What the Gospel forever takes away from Christians is the right to judge between the worthy and the unworthy poor." When we sit in judgment like that, we stand aloof and apart. That's precisely the position the Gospel does not allow a Christian—as if we could critique who is worthy and who is unworthy. Our criteria will always be cultural and too often self-interested.

A person might be at fault to some degree, but poverty is primarily a psychological state to which one surrenders after repeatedly being put down. It's a state of oppression. After continually being assaulted by negative voices from within or without, finally we surrender to them. We can't stand against them. Soon we are so disadvantaged that we can't even recognize, much less take advantage of, the opportunities offered to us. The negative voices of cultural shame soon become self-fulfilling prophecies.

People who have never been in this downtrodden, impoverished situation can be very unsympathetic because they don't realize what's happening inside. From their secure position—usually in the middle or upper classes—it's easy to call the poor lazy or unmotivated. Such people do not understand the psychological dimension of poverty. The poor have little chance of changing their state without some help from outside. Some "good news"!

This state is often characterized by what is called "victim behavior." It's self-destructive and other-destructive, and it characterizes all oppressed people. Those who are not in such a state of oppression cannot understand their behavior. It doesn't fit their criteria, so they misjudge and misinterpret almost everything the disadvantaged do.

Victim behavior is predictable. It is deadly. And it characterizes much, if not most, of the human race in one form or another. We may all be thinking of some group other than ourselves, but every group finds itself in that state of oppression in relation to some other group.

A CHILD'S TOTAL FAITH

Trusting in God is not a passive dependency, a handing over of responsibility: "Okay, God, you can do it." Faith in God is primarily an active virtue. Faith does not necessarily mean an expectation that God will intervene. Faith is an end in itself. Faith is an active empowering of the other to be everything he or she can be for you. It calls forth in the other and in oneself what it sees. Some would simply call it "the power of positive thinking" or self-fulfilling trust.

Those who are parents can probably relate to this definition. That little baby you were holding looked up at you with total faith and expectation. It had faith in you. You became a mother because the child made you into a mother; the child actively empowered you to be everything you could be for it. Between the years when your children were one and six, you became capable of almost totally losing yourself in them. It's unbelievable what mothers go through, running constantly all day. Would you ever have thought you could lose yourself that way? You did it because you were the object of your child's faith. Only a child's faith in you and a child's need of

25

you could bring that incredible power and dedication out of a human being.

The faith of the blind man, saying, "Jesus, I need you, I love you, I want you" becomes the channel of trust and openness through which the power of Jesus can flow to heal that person and change that person's life. This is one of the most central things about faith that I can say. It is a quality of relationship that works "magic."

THE FORGIVENESS PATH OF THE SAINTS

Even with all the best intentions in the world, given our different temperaments, backgrounds, and the way we process our data and information, we are going to step on one another's toes. Two people with absolutely good will can deeply hurt one another. Good people hurt one another because we all come at reality in different ways. That's why, for Jesus, the only way to achieve union is through forgiveness, not through making sin impossible.

We might think that the only way to achieve union is to gather together a group of absolutely good and healed people or excommunicate nonconformists. But truth is deeper than that. Jesus says the only way to achieve union is through failure, vulnerability, and repair—because people are always going to hurt one another. I wish authors would write realistically about lives of the saints, so we'd know that. Until the day they died, they had been doing things at which you and I would be scandalized. No person in the Bible, not even Jesus and Mary, would pass the strange litmus tests for holiness instituted later. The Bible presents real people who make real mistakes and work through them with God's help. (For example, both Moses and St. Paul were known murderers.)

You are on the same forgiveness path as the saints. The same Spirit is at work freeing you, you are struggling with the same difficulties they had, and you are learning both to receive and grant a universal forgiveness. This is the sum and substance of Jesus' teaching. If you don't "get" forgiveness, you don't get the core message.

MISSING THE MARK

For many people today the concept of "sin" has become hard to understand—the very word stirs up resistance. The church's doctrine of sin has often been used to intimidate people. Above all, the church's sexual morality was for centuries presented in a way that led to a thousand anxieties, repressions, and guilt feelings. This might suggest that we should just do without the word altogether. But that produces a vacuum that can't be filled in any other way. It is more meaningful to learn to understand the term in a new way. The Greek word for "sin," *hamartia*, comes from the art of archery and actually means "missing the mark." Sinning in this sense means going wide of the target. That was what Augustine had in mind when he said, "Seek what you are seeking—but don't seek it where you are seeking it!" The German word for sin,

Sünde, contains the root *sund* (English "sunder"), which means "cleft" or "separation." The word "sin" therefore means our separation from God, but also from our fellow human beings and from ourselves.

Sins are fixations that prevent the energy of life, God's love, from flowing freely. This can be illustrated in particular by fear. Fear is not a moral category, but it can stand between us and God, and thus hinder love and life.... Sins are attempts to cope with or enhance life with unsuitable means. Sins are a kind of misleading packaging: they make a promise that they can't keep. Although our sin is in part a reaction to other people's guilt, we have "chosen" it; we cling stubbornly to it and are responsible for it. So long as we blame others and don't take responsibility for our own lives, the separation can't be overcome. We remain trapped.

A FAVORITE VICE

With each of us there is a key dilemma, a main root of evil, a favorite vice. It colors and flavors all areas of our life. This one pitfall is so present in our lives that we ourselves do not recognize it. We were always this way. That's why we have to try to catch it "on the run," so to speak. As a rule, it's a great Aha! experience. At a stroke it becomes clear why I've done everything that I've done. I see that I had the same behavior models in place even as a little boy. It's the crimson thread that runs through my life. It explains everything: why I chose certain friends, why I played a certain sport or why I didn't, and so on. The crimson thread runs everywhere. Realizing and admitting this is actually more than sobering. "I did all the right things for the wrong reasons!"

OUR GIFT IS OUR SIN

Our sin and our unredeemed perception of the world are, paradoxically, the methods that helps us get to our driving force. When we commit our "favorite sin," we are, so to speak, "fully there." That is why we can't simply give it up: it belongs to the specific way that we give our life a goal and a direction. It belongs to the survival strategy that we adopted as children. We're all creatures of habit. We keep retreating back to where we feel at home. That is why we will find our gift where our sin is.

RECOGNIZING OUR PASSIONS

Why in our encounter with life do we human beings so often keep running up against ourselves instead of making a breakthrough to God, to the Totally Other? In our present-day egocentric society, we are especially inclined to remain stuck in our own thoughts or feelings. For this reason, for many Westerners, unless they have dismissed God completely, God today is nothing more than a projected image of themselves: a God that we desire, fear, or culturally need. The encounter with the Totally Other, with the Not-I, does not take place for most people.

The old masters and spiritual guides wanted people to acknowledge their blockages and prejudices, or their mode of perception—that is, their habitual way of viewing and shaping life from an egocentric viewpoint. In the Middle Ages, such compulsions were called passions. Unrecognized "passions" allow me to mistake my limited perspective for the whole. The task is to overcome these passions and to learn to perceive reality (more) objectively. We have to press through to God, the Totally Objective, who for Christians is at the same time Totally Ours, since he has committed himself to our world and become part of it. We must be capable of meeting someone other than ourselves.

THE DARKNESS IS A PART OF US

I have a rule of thumb that says that those who believe they are holy aren't. Jesus said that the prostitutes, the tax collectors, and the sinners would enter the Reign of God rather than those who sit before him in the synagogue. When Jesus healed sick people, he always said, "Your faith has made you whole." He never said, "Your correct doctrine, your orthodoxy, your dogmatism have healed you."

I too hope, of course, that I'm acting correctly, but I can't continually circle around this question. The problem is precisely in the need to be right and the need to think of myself as right. That is the problem for the soul. I have to do my work and leave the judgment to God. I need to avoid the compulsion to constantly pass judgment, because those who constantly pass judgment are not in a position to honestly perceive their own reality.

Naturally we have to learn to distinguish between darkness and light. But we dare not succumb to the illusion that we ourselves don't have a share in the darkness. The darkness we see is always a part of us. We can't naively skip over the subject of darkness and light. And it's precisely because we were so naive that we so often became victims of dark powers and called them light. I tell people who want to be prophets: you can't play the prophet until you've discovered in yourself what you accuse others of.

BEYOND AN ALL-OR-NOTHING OUTLOOK

More than with any other personality trait in my life, all-or-nothing thinking has caused me to make huge mistakes and bad judgments, hurt people and myself, withhold love, and misinterpret situations. And this pattern of dualistic or polarity thinking is deeply entrenched in most Western people, despite its severe limitations. Binary thinking is not wrong or bad in itself—in fact, it is necessary in most situations. But it is completely inadequate for the major questions and dilemmas of life.

Why do we do this to ourselves and one another? Don't I know that every viewpoint is a view from a point? Why can't I stand back and observe that I always have a preference or bias

or need, perhaps even a good and helpful one? Don't I know by now that some of the information is never all of the information? What is it that makes it so hard to backtrack from my position once I've declared it in my mind, and especially if I declare it publicly?

The ability to stand back and calmly observe my inner dramas, without rushing to judgment, is foundational for spiritual seeing. It is the primary form of "dying to the self" that Jesus lived personally and the Buddha taught experientially. The growing consensus is that, whatever you call it, such calm, egoless seeing is invariably characteristic of people at the highest levels of doing and loving in all cultures and religions. They are the ones we call sages or wise women or holy men. They see like the mystics see.

THE DISGUISES OF THE FALSE SELF

"We don't teach meditation to the young monks.
They are not ready for it until they stop slamming doors."

—*Thich Nhat Hanh to Thomas Merton in 1966*

The piercing truth of this statement struck me as a perfect way to communicate the endless disguises and devices of the false self. There is no more clever way for the false self to hide itself than behind the mask of spirituality. And the more mature the spiritual mask looks, the more dangerous it is. Thus things like professional religious roles, honorific titles, special clothing, any disciplined practice or asceticism, all visible shows of piety have always been seen as risky at best by spiritual teachers; Jesus himself warns against them and avoids them personally *(see Matt. 6:1–6; 11:18–19; 23:1–12).*

But these ego-masks take a new form in every age. It is easy and even trendy to bash public religious roles, but it is very hard to critique the current movements of "spirituality": specialized forms of prayer, new up-to-date postures and teachers, and especially any form of meditation or contemplation. They can also be used by the unstable ego to give itself identity, self-image, definition, and power.

The human ego will always try to name, categorize, fix, control, and ensure all its experiences. For the ego everything is a commodity. It lives inside of self-manufactured boundaries instead of inside the boundaries of the Godself. It lives out of its own superior image instead of mirroring the image of God. With the Western isolated self in a state of immense insecurity today, we are flailing about, searching for any solid identity. "Why not see myself as an enlightened person? Why not read the appropriate authors and attend the appropriate workshops? Why not try on the 'spiritual' persona?" We can thus concoct a quick "salvation," without ever really growing up or "dying" to our false selves at all. A spiritual self-image gives us status, stability, and security. There is no better way to remain unconscious than to baptize and bless mere form instead of surrendering to the deeper substance. I know this because I have done it myself.

Spiritual seeking, when it is done by the false self, might be the biggest problem of all. In the name of seeking God, the ego just pads and protects itself, which is an almost perfect cover for its inherent narcissism.

LASTING LOVE

Looking over the last decades of American culture, I think the reason that the hippie gospel of love was so hollow and did not bear fruit or last very long was because it lacked the necessary prior stage of repentance and conversion. When you preach love without conversion, you don't get lasting love. If you don't first call people to grow, to change, to call themselves into question, to be willing to go to a new level of consciousness, you can't sustain love for very long. In fact, you don't get genuine love at all. You get a temporary, make-believe, romantic, idealized experience, like the "love" young people often get caught up in: they wish to be in love and fantasize what it would be like to be in love. Or they repeat the love messages they hear in their songs: "Love is all you need." "Love is everything." "Love is the answer."

We can all agree with those slogans, but if you just preach them apart from conversion, change, and repentance, you are not preaching a credible or sustainable message.

THE RESULT OF EXCESS

Excess turns all gifts into curses.

CONTACT WITH THE NUMINOUS

Toward the end of his career Carl Jung said that he was not aware of a single one of his patients in the second half of their lives whose problem could not have been solved by contact with the "numinous" or the Absolute Center *(Letters, vol. 1, 1973, p. 377)*. An extraordinary statement from a man who considered himself alienated from institutional religion! Yet decades later we find ourselves condemned to live in a world in which "the best lack all conviction and the worst are full of passionate intensity." The Center has not held. Most of the gods we have met in our narcissistic age have been no more than projected and magnified images of ourselves. The Catholic God looks Roman, the charismatic God looks sweet, the liberal God looks undemanding, and the American God looks tribal and pathetic.

We wait for the Word of the Lord. We wait for the season of the Word of the Lord. The falcon must hear the falconer.

STEALING THE FIRE

If Someone is not holding together the Big World, then I had best concentrate on making sense out of my own little corner. If No One else is finally in charge, I had best take charge. If No One else is caring for me, I had better be preoccupied with security and insurance. If No One else is naming me, I will be very invested in my own image. If the only joy is self-acquired, then any mood-altering substance will do. All the burden, anxiety, and options are back on me, and I must take myself too seriously. It is the glory and the price of secular men and women. When Prometheus can no longer enjoy sitting at the fireplace of the gods, he must steal his own fire, but he pays the price forever. Such seems our contemporary exile. The human mind is enamored and burdened with itself, trying desperately to hold itself together. Trapped in our fractured worlds, we are unable to reconnect with one another.

THE CENTER CANNOT HOLD

Living in this material world, with a physical body and in a culture of affluence that rewards the outer self, it is both more difficult to know our spiritual self and all the more necessary. Our skin-encapsulated egos are the only self that we know and therefore our only beginning place. But they are not the only or even the best place. That is our contemporary dilemma: (1) Our culture no longer values the inner journey. (2) We actively avoid and fear it. (3) In most cases we no longer even have the tools to go inward because (4) we are enamored of and entrapped in the private ego and its private edges. In such a culture, "The center cannot hold," at least for long.

JESUS BUILT CIRCLES, NOT PYRAMIDS

Pyramids are always pyramids of sacrifice. Whether it is the hundreds of thousands of slaves creating monuments to Egyptian kings, the sacrificial victims offering their hearts to Aztec gods, or the underpaid maids and janitors in the tourist hotels of the world, someone always has to give his life or her life so that someone else can be "special." When that specialness is idealized and protected, instead of avoided and made unnecessary as Jesus taught, we have the destructive and dark side of power. Jesus struck at the nerve center of all of these when he empowered honest human relationships instead of degrees of religious worthiness. Jesus built circles instead of pyramids.

What they could not forgive him for, even on the cross, was that he announced the necessary destruction of the holy temple. "Not a stone will stand on a stone. Everything will be destroyed" *(Mark 13:2)*.

A SELF TRANSFORMED

There has to be some degree of withdrawal from the revolving hall of mirrors in order to find oneself primarily mirrored by God. This is an urgent need, not just for me personally, but also for a culture that seems lost in monthly media dramas, projections, and conversations that merely fill up the time and temporarily assuage the loneliness. We feel socially contagious today, and no one is benefiting from it: "Sound and fury, signifying nothing." We tend to mirror group feelings instead of knowing who we really are.

We thought that if we stopped believing in God we would be free from belief. But instead we believe in everything! Conspiracy theories, medical treatments, fundamentalism from anywhere except Christianity, power in stars and plants, and crystals, apparitions, and dogmatism seem to be everywhere.

Our culture and frankly much of our peace and justice work is dominated by very fragile egos, superficial intellectual and emotional lives, knee-jerk reactions that are often politically correct but nowhere close to the Gospel. As I wrote in my hermitage journal, "The self that begins the journey is not the self that arrives at the Gospel. The self that begins is the self that we think ourselves to be, the superior self we want to be. This is the self that dies along the way— until 'no one' is left. This is the true self that all Great Religion talks about, the self bigger than death yet born of death, a different self than the private I, a self transformed by God and transformed in God."

ANAWIM: THE POOR

Jesus' harshest words are aimed at hypocrites, and the second harshest at the people who are primarily concerned with possessions. He says that power, prestige, and possessions are the three things that prevent us from recognizing and receiving the Reign of God. When he says that to good, upright people, they react with indignation and consider his remarks scandalous. They call him an unbeliever, an enemy of the law, and finally a devil—because they own too many things that they now must defend. The only ones who can accept the proclamation of the Reign are those who have nothing to protect, not their own self-image or their reputation, their possessions, their theology, their principles, or their certitudes. And these are called "the poor," *anawim* in Hebrew.

ACKNOWLEDGING YOUR FEAR

I don't advise trying to master fears. You can't fix the soul. You can only acknowledge your own rage and your fear of trusting and refuse to identify with it.

THE THREE DEMONS IN THE WILDERNESS

There are three primary things that we have to let go of. First is the compulsion to be successful. Second is the compulsion to be right—even, and especially, to be theologically right. . . . Finally there is the compulsion to be powerful, to have everything under control. I'm convinced that these are the three demons Jesus faced in the wilderness. And so long as we haven't looked these three demons in the face, we should presume that they're still in charge. The demons have to be called by name, clearly, concretely, and practically, spelling out just how imperious and self-righteous we are.

WHEN RELIGION CANNOT KNEEL

Aristotle said democracy would only work in a culture already committed to virtue. There is no communal myth left that teaches us the essentially tragic nature of human life; there is no vision that proclaims the primacy of the common good; there is no transcendent image that makes human virtue a divine reflection. There is No One to reflect and No One to love and serve. I do not want to belong to a religion that cannot kneel. I do not want to live in a world where there is No One to adore. It is a lonely and labored world if I am its only center. My life is too short to discover wisdom on my own, to identify and properly name my own self-importance, to learn how to love if I have to start at zero.

WE MUST LOVE THEM BOTH

I doubt whether a single cultural myth or national story is now possible. That is frightening as we experience the fractured results while groups divide, encircle, and defend.... The rifts and chasms are irreparable. Many are unable to offer one another basic respect, engage in civic dialogue, or honor what God is apparently patient with: the human struggle.... But I am still advised by Thomas Aquinas, who said, "We must love them both: those whose opinions we share and those whose opinions we reject. For both have labored in search for their truth and both have helped us in the finding of our own."

FINDING A DEEP YES

You cannot make an art form out of critique itself; it is not the kind of deep passion or positive faith that can stand up to war, or vengeance, or long-haul injustice. It hooks the negative voices inside of all of us, which the young especially do not yet need. They have not yet found a truly positive vision. You have to be able to find a deep yes before you can dare to say no.

JOY IN IMPERFECTION

Christian maturity is the ability to joyfully live in an imperfect world.

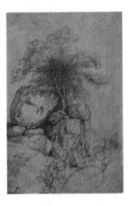

Part Three

FROM PROFOUND SUFFERING
COME GREAT WISDOM AND JOY

It is the things that you cannot do anything about and the things that you cannot do anything with that do something with you.

SUFFERING AND PRAYER:
THE TWO GOLDEN PATHS

Faith demands living with a certain degree of anxiety and holding a very real amount of tension. We have to be trained how to do this. The only two things that are strong enough to accomplish this training are suffering and prayer. These two golden paths lead to a different shape of meaning, a different-sized universe, a different set of securities and goals, and always a different Center. Only suffering and prayer are strong enough to decentralize both the ego and the superego. The practice of prayer, we can choose to do ourselves; the suffering is done to us. But we have to be ready to learn from it when it happens and not waste time looking for someone to blame for our unnecessary suffering. That takes some good and strong teaching, too. As I love to say, "It is the things that you cannot do anything about and the things that you cannot do anything with that do something with you."

WHENEVER WE SEE TRUE PAIN

Would there be communion at all if there were no need on this earth, no suffering on this earth? If there were no sin?

No imperfection? I think there would be no such communion as we now have. We would each live in our isolated worlds. I would not need you. I would not be drawn to you. I would be self-sufficient. I would be caught up smugly and happily in my own perfection. I would simply draw my life totally from within and would never need to look at the beauty or pain on others' faces. This is the Gnostic temptation, condemned in some form in every century. There are two things that draw us outside of ourselves: pain on other people's faces, and the unbelievable beauty that is other human beings at their best. Or in other words: cross and resurrection.

Pain and beauty constitute the two faces of God. Unbelievable beauty, on the one hand, that we see reflected in the beauty of human beings to which we forever find ourselves attracted—whether it be physical beauty or spiritual beauty. But, on the other hand, mysteriously, brokenness, lameness, and weakness also pull us out of ourselves. We feel them both together in the case of a child. All a helpless child has to do is raise up its hands and most of us go rushing to help.

That factor of vulnerability forces us beyond ourselves. Whenever we see true pain, most of us are drawn out of our own preoccupations and want to take away the pain. I think we are rushing not just toward the hurt child, we are rushing toward God. Toward the suffering God. We want to take the suffering in our arms. That's why Francis could kiss the leper. That's why so many saints wanted to get near suffering—because, as they said again and again, they met Christ there. It "saved" them from their smaller and untrue self.

Many who are working among the suffering or poor say the same. They thought they were going as the benefactors, but they invariably found themselves being helped and liberated. We are saved by those whom we go to save, and both of us are then saved in spite of ourselves. There is a mysterious "third" who is doing the saving. Suffering for and with the other seems to be the only way we know that our lives are not about us.

YOU MUST DRINK OF THE CUP

Jesus told the first disciples, "You do not know what you are asking. Until you drink of the cup that I must drink, and be baptized with the baptism that I will be immersed in" (Mark 10:38), you really do not know what I am talking about. You have nothing to say. It is not that we have a message and then suffer for it. It is much more the opposite: We suffer, come through it transformed, and then we have a message! This is the clear Jesus pattern and why he trained his disciples in the necessary path of suffering. There is something, it seems, that we can know in no other way. We hope to bypass such suffering by being moral, by being orthodox, by being ritualistic, but his words remain the same to us: "The cup that I must drink, you must also drink" *(Mark 10:39)*.

Enlightenment, conversion, and seeing the truth is a journey of transformation, not a matter of membership in the right group or reciting the correct formulas or even practicing the right morality. As Paul made so clear both in his letters to the Romans and to the Galatians, law can give you correct information, but only God's Spirit of love can transform you.

GOD GETS CLOSER
BLOW BY BLOW

The word of God calls us to greater wisdom. The only way the Lord can do so is by making the system fall apart. That's called suffering. It's how God shows us that life is always bigger than we presently imagine it. Faith allows us deliberately to live in a shaky position so that we have to rely upon Another. God gets closer blow by blow.

WHEN YOU HAVE NO CONTROL

Jesus named control and domination as the false form of power. "Among pagans it is the kings who lord it over them.... This must not happen with you!" *(Luke 22:25–26)*. But then he continues by unapologetically contrasting it with true power: "You who stand faithfully with me through trials ... You will sit on thrones to judge the twelve tribes of Israel" *(Luke 22:28, 30)*. The power that Jesus trusts and offers is precisely the power that comes to us through the suffering of powerlessness, the power that is found when you have no control at all.

THE SPACE OF NONANSWER

"I know it is as you say. How can man be in the right against God? ... His heart is wise, and his strength is great. Who then can successfully defy him?" *(Job 9:1, 4)*. I know I don't have a chance, Job is saying, I know God is right somehow; I just don't understand in this instance how he's right. But I'm willing to wait.

That's the difference. He's willing to wait in that space of nonanswer. That's the space in which God creates faith.

SYMBOLS THAT HEAL

Two words of Greek origin are important at this stage: "symbolic" and "diabolic." Symbolic means to throw together. Diabolic means to throw apart. Evil is always dualistic, always separates: body from soul, heart from head, human from divine, masculine from feminine. Whenever we separate, evil comes into the world.

People I have known with psychotic or neurotic problems invariably have been emotionally divided. One part of their emotional life is affirmed, another part repressed—don't think that, don't feel that. Thus, one part of their humanity is denied. We all find myriad ways to divide, to separate: "You're not an acceptable person because of your color or religion or race." Whenever we divide, we destroy.

Symbolism, however, always reconnects what has been thrown apart. This probably explains why healthy religion (re-ligio: to bind back together) throughout history gives us symbols, images of reconciliation, that heal, that put together what has been taken apart.... God is always the great reconciler and healer of opposites—even sin and goodness.

RESURRECTION TAKES CARE OF ITSELF

It is not quick or easy, we find, to allow the true self or to allow the true God. The task of life is the gradual unveiling of both.... Resurrection takes care of itself. It comes naturally once the false self is abandoned. But what an abandoning! Every movement toward union will feel like a loss of self-importance and self-control.

WHEN SOMEONE CARRIES
THE BURDEN WITH US

In the spiritual life it's much more important to know how to listen than to know how to talk.

Most of us are not trained in redemptive listening. We're trained to give answers. In the counseling context, this listening mode is often called nondirective counseling. It is based on the premise that one can't ultimately provide the answers for others. All one can do is walk with the other and help others rightly to hear themselves. What people long to have happen is to be somehow received, understood. When they are heard, it seems, they can begin to hear. The most redemptive thing one can do for another is just to understand.

No one but God can capture the full projection of one's soul. When we're young, we try to fall in love with the perfect person who will totally understand us, and the great disappointment is to discover that no one person can. . . .

When we are understood, when we feel another person really cares, it's surprising how the problem, for the most part, can fade. We don't need the answer anymore. The mere fact that someone is carrying the burden with us, walking with us on the journey (for some unbelievable reason—it's not logical at all), takes care of much of the problem.

SHARING IN SUFFERING

For sixteen hundred years we have had the church for the poor. It was always thought grand and glorious that our saints and religious founders would go and help the poor. We thank God for Mother Teresa. But most of the rest of us felt entitled to live undisturbed in our established and wealthy private worlds.

A wonderful conversion is now happening in all the churches. Unable to become the church of the poor, we at least are trying to be the church with the poor. We are learning to stand more in solidarity with the outcasts of society and also to enjoy their privileged position in hearing the word of God.

Every real saint eventually left the system of possessions, privilege, and power, so that he or she could hear and speak the truth. In doing so, they were joining Jonah in the whale, Jeremiah in the cistern, Job on the dunghill, and Jesus on the cross. It seems to be the way.

WHEN YOU CANNOT FORGIVE

We stand as a people forgiven. That's essentially what Christians are: forgiven sinners— -not people who don't sin, but those who know they are forgiven, loved, and believed in. The very concrete practical corollary is that if we live in hatred and unforgiveness, we'll never be able to believe in God's forgiveness. Forgiving and being forgiven are two sides of one coin, so we ask God to "forgive us our sins as we forgive one another" *(Luke 11:3)*.

When you find yourself incapable of forgiving another person, that means you are not standing in the stream of God's forgiveness. Work backward. When you find your heart hardened and you cannot forgive, you're forgetting that God forgives you. But when you let your belief in God's forgiveness soften and free you, you find it easier to forgive others.

THE STORY OF THE TWO SONS
(THE PRODIGAL SON)

Luke 15:11–32 presents the story we've always called the Prodigal Son. This is not the best title. It might better be called the story of the Two Sons. It seems the story was told, first of all, to present the attitude of the elder son as the image of the usual church person: the obedient person ... "the one who never disobeyed your orders" *(v. 29)* but who will not come to the banquet.

The Prodigal Son might also be better called the story of the Merciful Father. It's a proclamation of the nature of God's love and mercy. It's interesting that we've emphasized the prodigal son, because he is the least important of the characters here. He's not the Everyman figure. We're all certainly prodigal sons, but the real Everyman figure is the righteous church person who gets upset at people who get saved after they've lived a whole life of sin.

"How can they be as good as I am? I've been going to Mass faithfully since I've been six years old. I always obey the law. And now these people come along being converted and dancing in the Spirit at age sixty, while I had to suffer all my life. Didn't my faithfulness get me any points with God?" In that context, God as the only faithful one becomes very apparent. God as the merciful father is clearly the protagonist and hero of the story.

An African missionary told me he found stories like the prodigal son in many African cultures. He told one from the tribe among whom he was working. He said it almost brought tears to his eyes when he first understood it, as it did for me.

In this tribe, the father-son relationship is absolutely essential to the perpetuation of the culture. In no way can that relationship be tampered with or destroyed, otherwise everything falls apart. The son has to be faithful to his father and the father has to be faithful to his son.... If the son breaks the relationship, leaves his home, or is mad at his father, the father does one thing immediately. He goes to the mountains to pray. He remains in prayer asking God for the "spittle of forgiveness."

... The father remains in the mountains, praying for the spittle of forgiveness. This says something important about sacramentalism, for when the son does decide to return home after he's sown his wild oats or rebelled, runners go to the mountain to tell the father his son is returning. These runners accompany the father down the mountain, and another contingent accompanies the son.

... Here are the two teams coming together, the father with the runners coming down from the mountain and the other group coming with the son. They meet and, of all things, what the father does is spit on his son's face. Among us, that would be a sign of contempt. For them, however, it is giving to the son what is from inside the father, the

spit that symbolizes himself. The running of the father's spit over the son's face is their deepest symbol of forgiveness. Throughout this culture, spit is constantly used as a symbol of forgiveness.

... I use that African story as another example of the same kind of story Jesus is trying to tell in the parable of the Two Sons. Jesus uses the precious relationship between the father and the son as an image of the God/person relationship. Most commentators agree that this story expresses the true spirit and style of the historical Jesus. In this quintessential Jesus sermon, he is saying that God takes the initiative, God is the lover, God loves unconditionally, God knows we've sinned, but God comes running out after us.

SOON WE'LL ALL BE GONE

The call of the Lord is always to live in the present. Suppose we knew for certain the date that the world was going to end. What would we do differently, except, I hope, to continue what we are already doing?

If the only way we can motivate people to live a life of goodness is to talk about end times, then they are not motivated at all. If people are following the Lord only because the world is going to end, then they're not really following the Lord. They're simply trying to avoid disaster. We need lovers, delighters, positive builders—not dour naysayers.

To assert that the world is going to end is not morbid teaching, however; it's realistic. To live as if your life is not going to end is to live a lie. To pretend that life will go on forever is precisely that, a pretense. By the year 2150, none of us alive today will be walking this earth anymore.

. . . Some of us will be talked about, but most of us will be forgotten. Soon we'll all be gone. Remembering this keeps us not only from taking ourselves too seriously, but it also helps us take ourselves very seriously. That's why the Gospel was always presented in that tension of the end time.

. . . You and I are going to die. . . .

When your whole life passes before you, no single thing is really that important. In other words, don't sell your soul for winning one petty argument or resolving one little situation or overcoming one minor pain—don't let that single moment, no matter how important it may seem to you now, control the rest of your life.

. . . When you realize that everything is important, and yet it is all passing away, then no individual event matters that much. You can let it go.

SPIRITUALITY AND PAIN

All great spirituality is about what we do with our pain.

LETTING GO OF EMOTIONS

Emotions have an important function in the spiritual life, but we shouldn't become dependent on them. And we should not strive for them for their own sake. We experience a purification through trials, so that we can be freed from our attachment to feelings and not take the transitory emotions too seriously. We have to let go of them, so that really great emotions can come to light, genuine passions that free us for leading a completely different life.

Normally it goes like this: The more we grow in faith, the fewer emotional experiences we'll have. Teresa of Avila, who has written such wonderful things about the dark night of purification, says that she spent eighteen years without one comforting emotion. But afterward she experienced quite deep ecstatic feeling. Many of us are so emotionally

overstimulated—we watch so many movies, we hear so much music—that we're no longer capable of the deeper feelings. We're not prepared for the feelings that really convert and change us. That is why some sort of "fasting" experience is so important for us. That's the meaning and the original significance of the forty days of Lent.

MISERY

The Spirit of truth will always set you free, but first it will make you miserable.

ALLOWING THE DARK SIDE

Any allowing of the hidden side of things, the dark side of things—while also holding onto the attractive and knowable side—usually marks the beginning of nondual consciousness. Whenever we can appreciate the value of something, while still knowing its limitations and failures, this also marks the beginning of wisdom and nondual consciousness.

Most humans are not very good at such "allowing"; it often feels like what Paul calls "groaning." In recent centuries, no one has shown us exactly how to do this. Perhaps a more familiar word is simply "forgiveness." The struggle to forgive reality for being exactly what it is right now often breaks us through to nondual consciousness. We have to overcome the rational domination of ego and reason to forgive a deep hurt of memory. As Zachariah says in his beautiful canticle, "You will know salvation through the mystery of forgiveness" *(Luke 2:77)*. That's it!

THE THIN LINE
BETWEEN JOY AND SUFFERING

The more deeply we enter into the mystery of Christ, the thinner becomes the line between joy and suffering, according to people who have gone down that road. Such people sometimes have to think twice to realize whether they are feeling joy or sorrow. Once the heart has surrendered, the only important question becomes: Are we doing God's will? Whether it brings us personal happiness or sadness is no longer of primary importance.

JOY AND PAIN: A LESSON FROM
MERTON'S HERMITAGE

Some years ago my Franciscan superiors gave me a year's leave to spend in contemplation. I know it was a great privilege, and it struck me as a luxury. As a motto for this "sabbatical" I chose the maxim of the Austrian philosopher Ludwig Wittgenstein: "Don't think. Just look." I decided to fast from books, radio, and TV, so as not to take in any more information and ideas. I wanted to try to get a good clear look at what I had already experienced and lived until then.

I didn't need any fresh information; I had to learn to reflect upon previous experiences, to chew them thoroughly. I had to taste on my tongue their positive and their negative sides, their sweetness and their bitterness.

I had previously given a retreat for a Trappist monastery, where the abbot asked me whether he could do me a favor. I asked him to allow me to live for thirty days in the hermitage of the famous poet-monk Thomas Merton, who died in 1968. I had read the books of Thomas Merton and was very enthusiastic about him; he was my model. I thought that if I were at his place, I might be able to absorb some of his wisdom. And so I managed to spend the spring in the hills of Kentucky, absolutely alone with myself, with the woods, and, I hoped, with God. I thought beforehand that it would probably be deadly boring. I wondered what I'd do all day long. I put my chair in front of the door and watched the sun come up in the morning. And in the late afternoon I placed my chair on the other side of the hut and watched the sun go down.

I tried to keep a diary of what was happening to me. Because I'm a man and because I'm of German extraction, I find it particularly hard to cry. But one evening I laid my finger on my cheek and found to my surprise that it was wet. I wondered what those tears meant. What was I crying for? I wasn't consciously sad at all or consciously happy. I noticed at this moment that behind it all there was a joy, deeper than any private joy. It was a joy in the face of the beauty of being, a joy at all the wonderful and lovable people I had already met in my life. Cosmic or spiritual joy is something you participate in; it comes from elsewhere and flows through you, and it has little or nothing to do with things going well in your own life at that moment. Thus the saints would rejoice in the midst of suffering, which to the rest of us is unthinkable.

But at the same moment I experienced exactly the opposite emotion. I hadn't known that two such contrary feelings could coexist. The tears were at the same time tears of an immense sadness—a sadness at what we're doing to the earth, sadness at the people whom I have already hurt in my life, and a sadness too at my own emptiness and stupidity. And even today, years after this experience, I still don't know whether joy or pain had the upper hand—they lay so close to each other.

GOD IS PARTICIPATING WITH US

The enfleshment and suffering of Jesus tell us that God is not apart from the trials of humanity. God is not aloof. God is not a mere spectator. God is participating with us. God is not merely tolerating human suffering or healing suffering. God is participating with us in it. That is what gives believers both meaning and hope.

Part Four
THE MYSTICAL PATH IS A
CELEBRATION OF PARADOX

GOD IS THE LIGHT
THAT DWELLS IN DARKNESS

God is light, yet this light seems to dwell in darkness. We must go into this darkness to see the light. Our age, however, resists the language of "descent." We belong to an age and culture that have been able to manufacture a kind of "ascent" unlike that of our ancestors. Reason, medicine, technology, and speed have allowed us to avoid the ordinary "path of the fall." Now we are unpracticed and afraid.

PERFECTLY HIDDEN AND PERFECTLY REVEALED

God has written the patterns in things as they are, and yet we never see the full pattern without divine assistance. God seems to be both perfectly hidden and perfectly revealed in all things. Thus, faith (trust in the other) is always necessary to see what is then "natural." What a paradox!

PARADOXES IN ENDLESS EMBRACE

True participation in paradox liberates us from our own control towers and for the compelling and overarching vision of the Reign of God—where there are no liberals or conservatives. Here, the paradoxes—life and death, success and failure, loyalty to what is and risk for what needs to be—do not fight with one another, but lie in an endless embrace. We must penetrate behind them both—into the mystery that bears them both.3

WHO YOU THINK GOD IS, GOD ISN'T

Jesus doesn't fit. Even after two thousand years, it is hard to realize what a revolutionary symbol, revelation, and reality Jesus is. He basically turned theology upside down. He said, in effect: Who you think God is, God isn't. You can't know this merely by study or theology or religion, but only through painful encounters with the living God where you feel your flesh being torn off and yet you do not die. Then you experience another kind of life, another kind of freedom. Christians call it the life of the risen Jesus. . . .

This may explain why the people who have met Jesus are humble people. Because they have been overwhelmed by a humble God. A God who is not overwhelming and triumphant, with all the answers and all the perfection, but a God who is somehow in this with us. A God who is infinite, yet somehow finite. Who is in charge, yet chooses not to be in control at all.

CARRYING THE DILEMMA

In India I felt that there was no way to avoid the human dilemma through the usual means of mental gymnastics, political posturing, or projection of the shadow elsewhere. The dilemma is right there, glaring, obvious, overwhelming, and tragic. One either carries it or goes crazy. It is no surprise to me that the Indian culture was the matrix for both Gandhi and Mother Teresa. Only this many-thousand-year-old culture, the home of the world's oldest religions, has the depth to rediscover the nonviolent teaching of Jesus and the Great Compassion of God. Neither Gandhi nor Teresa looked for winners and losers; neither led us out of the human dilemma and "solved" our problems in any way. But just like Jesus, they led us directly into the human dilemma and agreed to carry it. These are the true "sons and daughters of God"!

WORDS BECOME FLESH

For saints, mystics, and budding contemplatives, "Words have become flesh," and experience has gone beyond words. Experience is always nondual, an open field. As St. Paul put it, "My spirit is praying, but my mind is left barren" *(1 Cor. 14:14)*. Words are mere guideposts now, and you recognize that most people have made them into hitching posts. Inside of such broad and deep awareness, paradoxes are easily accepted, and former mental contradictions seem to dissolve. That's why mystics can forgive and let go and show mercy and love enemies.

PARABLES AND KOANS

Jesus said that it took "parables" to subvert our unconscious worldview—and thereby expose its illusions, even to us. Parables should make us a bit uncomfortable if we are really "hearing" them. If we fit them nicely into our business-as-usual world, parables have not served their purpose. A parable is supposed to change our operative worldview and unlock it from the inside—so that we can see and hear reality correctly. New and full context allows us to read text truthfully. All religions have tried to do the same thing with riddles and koans and mythic stories. Our whole universe has to be rearranged truthfully before individual teachings can be heard correctly. What we have done for centuries in the West is give people new moral and doctrinal teaching without rearranging their mythic worldview. It does not work. It leads nowhere new—or nowhere truly old for that matter. It creates legalists, ritualists, minimalists, and literalists, who always kill the spirit of a thing (except in mathematics).

PARABLE: A CALL TO INSIGHT

A parable confronts our world and subverts it. It doesn't call for discussion, debate, or question; it is not God-as-information. Rather it is God-as-invitation-and-challenge. A parable calls us to insight and decision. A parable doesn't lead us to endless analysis; it's either a flashing insight or it's nothing. Like a joke, it leads up to the punch line. Either you get it or you don't.

A QUALITY OF MYSTERY

Untested faith tends to produce a very mechanistic and impersonal spirituality. Mature faith, however, almost always has a quality of paradox and mystery about it—as if to leave room for the freedom of God.

PARADOX AND AUTHENTIC SPIRITUALITY

Authentic spirituality is always paradoxical. I even think that any "common sense" that doesn't have a certain paradoxical character deserves to be distrusted. God takes me very seriously. But this frees me from the burden of having to do that chore myself. Perhaps it's a problem of semantics, but I can say that I take myself very seriously and at the same time not very seriously at all. And in the same moment both statements are entirely true.

HOW TO WIN BY LOSING

God saves humanity not by punishing it but by restoring it! We overcome our evil not by a frontal and heroic attack, but by a humble letting go that always first feels like losing.

Christianity is probably the only religion in the world that teaches us, from the very cross, how to win by losing. It is always a hard sell—especially for folks who are into strength, domination, winning, and enforcing conclusions. God's restorative justice is much more patient, and finally much more transformative, than mere coercive obedience.

WE ARE CHRIST'S BODY

We are not separate from Christ. We are his incarnation, his body. So our suffering is not separate; it is a continuation of the suffering of Christ that still endures for the life of the world. Much of Christianity has still not dealt with that. We still act as if Christ were "over there," and we are praying to Christ and pleasing Christ and trying to get Christ inside of us.

That's why I dislike such language as "I have accepted Christ into my heart as my personal savior." The implication is that we are actually separate and our brave decision changes all of that. The truth is that we are already in Christ by the power of the Spirit. We are his flesh, we are his body, we are his children. It's all a matter of recognition and response, which we call faith.

CONVERSION TO THE NO-ME

Conversion to the no-me . . . conversion to the other, the alien, the would-be enemy that we must learn to love. Men must be converted to the feminine and women to the masculine. Maybe that is why God made sexual attraction so compelling. If we are converted to the nonself, everything changes—in that it approaches authentic religious conversion (the utter no-me: God) more than any other type of conversion. From the whole—and Center—position, we see through eyes other than our own half-blinded ones. We see the other side of things and forgiveness becomes possible. We see that the enemy is not enemy but spiritual helpmate. There is nothing more to defend and nothing more to be afraid of once we have met and accepted our inner opposite. Not all opposites offer us possibility and transcendence.

MIRACLES ARE SIGNS

Two people can see a miracle. The one with faith will praise God; the one without will find some way to forget it or explain it away.... Miracles and signs don't produce people of deep faith, because invariably what such people want is another sign next Friday night to carry them through another week. That's the depth of their religion. For them, God is more like their private magician than someone they love and serve. Miracles, however, are signs for those who already have faith—faith that God is in all things.

PRAYING OUT LOUD

This I know: that my Avenger lives,
and he, the Last, will take his stand on earth.
After my awaking, he will set me close to him,
and from my flesh I shall look on God.
He whom I shall see will take my part:
these eyes will gaze on him and find him not aloof.
My heart within me sinks.

—Job 19:25–27

Where did Job's faith come from? How can Job rise to the occasion like this? His resurgence is built on no obvious human foundation. There is no antecedent. It's purely a creation of grace, as faith always is. It's a being lifted up by the hair and set down in a new place to do a new thing that surprises even ourselves. . . .

"Ah, would that these words of mine were written down . . . , would that they were inscribed on some monument with iron chisel and engraving tool, cut into the rock for ever" *(19:23–24)*. In this grandiose preface he is appealing to the future. He's not sure that even he can believe this now. He's not sure anybody else will believe it in the future. Humans use audiovisual aids like this when reality is getting out of control.

For example, when I'm not sure of my own prayer, I go to my journal. I want to write it so I can read it at a later time because I'm not sure that I mean it, although I want to mean it. Or I think that I mean it. Other times, when I particularly want to pray well, I go to a place where no one can hear me and I pray out loud so my own ears can hear it. I become a testimony to myself. That way, one is less likely to lie. You can't lie so comfortably when you pray out loud or when you write your prayer down.

LIMITLESS PRESENCE

If we gather all the Gospels together, we see that the teaching on the resurrection is not focused on the physical resuscitation of the body of Jesus. The resurrected body is an entirely new type of corporeality, a new type of bodiliness that is open to universal presence and yet is immediately available to one person. Jesus has become the all-available Christ. . . . At present, our human nature in its physical form is limited to a space-time continuum. My current body is a limited presence; if I'm here, I can't be there. That's not true of Jesus anymore. What the Gospels seem to be trying to say is that in the resurrection of the body we're seeing a new kind of bodiliness, a new kind of presence that is unlimited. Moreover, this limitless presence is a presence that is active and alive in each situation.

THE LAST WILL BE FIRST

Good theology is important. If I hadn't received good theology, I wouldn't have the authority to write this. But at the same time I'd like to stress how important spirituality is above everything else. And I'd like to reiterate that religion is one of the surest ways to avoid faith and to avoid God. That was demonstrated to us in the New Testament by the murder of Jesus. It was the priests and theologians who killed Jesus. The ones who accepted him were the lepers, the drunkards, and the prostitutes. Truth isn't where we suppose. As Jesus says, be prepared for the surprise that "the first will be last, and the last will be first" *(Matt. 19:30).*

OUR IMAGE OF GOD

Although priests know a great deal about theology, I've found to my surprise that their image of God is 90 percent a mixture of the image of their own mothers and fathers. And for some reason they themselves are always amazed when they discover this. If their mother was harshly critical, so is their God. If their father was distant and cold, likewise their God is distant and cold. I would encourage you to examine the extent to which this applies to your life as well.

Again, we have to break through the images to find who God really is. I promise you there's nothing to be afraid of here. But you have no basis to believe that until you take the journey yourself. People who pray always know that. People who empty themselves in the wilderness always meet a God who is greater than they would have dared to hope. The American Trappist monk Thomas Merton, a man who had a great deal of influence on me, describes this experience as "mercy, within mercy, within mercy."

HOW GOD COMES TO US

How does God come to each one of us? Sometimes God must come as a friend and at other times as a lover; at other times it may be good if God comes as a father. But if you

continue on your spiritual journey, I promise you that some
times God will reveal himself in feminine form: himself as
herself. And for some of us that may be the first time that we
fall in love with God.

Many people, I find, don't love God at all—maybe, even
most people; even very many religious people. To my surprise
I've discovered that many religious men and women even hate
God. Naturally they can't admit that to themselves. How
many people are afraid of God, how many experience God
as cold and absent, how many people have a sense of God as
someone who might toy with them or undercut them? They
have nothing to be afraid of. All we have to lose is that false
image that doesn't serve us, that image of ourselves that's
always too small and that image of God that's likewise too
small. We need to ask God to teach us to let go.

HEALING PHYSICAL AND SPIRITUAL

After Jesus cures a leper in Luke 5:12–16, his reputation
continues to grow, and large crowds gather to hear him and

be healed. His preaching is constantly mixed with healing. We do need those holistic signs of being free—cures and healings—not only in our minds and spirits but also in our bodies, memories, and emotions. That's the beauty of what we're coming to understand today about the full Gospel. God has come to free us at every level of our being.

BEYOND THE DEFENDED RITUAL

Christians kneel and raise hands, Buddhists sit in surrender, Muslims bow their heads to the earth many times a day, Natives whirl and dance before the Power, and Hindus burn incense and offer sacrifices. We are all fairly consistent with our rituals. We defend them and too often identify with them. But now we must go beyond the defended ritual to the Reality for which it stands.

PONTIFEX: THE BRIDGE BUILDER

The word pontifex means bridge-builder. The word is applied preeminently to the Holy Father: Pontifex Maximus means the greatest bridge-builder. History hints that the pope has not always been that, but the word shows that's what the early church expected from the bishop of Rome. I personally took great comfort from being a bridge-builder, connecting people who don't usually connect. I hoped new life would come out of that. But I learned after a while that you pay a price for being a bridge—people walk on you from both sides.

Both the right and the left, the capitalists and communists, however we describe the polarities—both sides use you for their own purposes. When you stand for the Gospel, you are in a very vulnerable position. Everybody thinks you're in it for ideology's sake. They want to put you in a box right away. Then inevitably you're seen to be in a box for the other side, and they hate you and presume you're wrong. . . .

The world is afraid of reconciliation. We prefer to live in a world of black and white where we create and maintain enemies, because that keeps our own group together. It has probably been this way since the beginning of time. Our human nature has trapped us in certain positions that have a degree of culture-forming logic to them but overall are simply untrue.

THE SIGN OF JONAH

Without the sign of Jonah—the pattern of new life only through death ("in the belly of the whale")—Christianity remains a largely impotent ideology, another way to "win" instead of the pain of faith. Or it becomes a language of ascent instead of the treacherous journey of descent that characterizes Jonah, Jeremiah, Job, John the Baptizer, and Jesus. After Jesus, we Christians used the metaphor "the way of the cross." Unfortunately, it became "what Jesus did to save us," or a negative theology of atonement, instead of the necessary pattern that is redemptive for all of us. Jesus became the cosmic problem-solver instead of the teacher of the path.

This one great truth has also been discovered by what we call Eastern religions: Taoism, yin and yang philosophy, the detachment of Buddhism, and the Hindu god of destruction and regeneration, Shiva. It is utterly surprising and disappointing that so many Christians think they are discovering this mystery for the first time in new religions. The Jonah-Job-Jesus pattern has been hard for Westerners to recognize and accept. There was probably a cultural resistance to it in the Greco-Roman West. where we were always focused on ascending and continual progress. The sign of Jonah is at the heart of the matter.

Part Five
CONTEMPLATION MEANS PRACTICING HEAVEN NOW

CONTEMPLATION, THE DIVINE THERAPY

By contemplation we mean the deliberate seeking of God through a willingness to detach from the passing self, the tyranny of emotions, the addiction to self-image, and the false promises of this world. It is a journey into faith and nothingness. The ordinary rules of thinking, managing, explaining, and fixing up the self do not apply here. It is a search for God, a love of larger Truth, and not the mere manipulation of ideas and feelings inside the private self. Contemplation is the "divine therapy" and the perennial clearinghouse for the soul. All the great world religions recognize its necessity in their more mature stages. For Christians, it is Jesus' sojourn in the desert for forty days and Mary's "Let it be done unto me according to your word" *(Luke 1:38)*.

We all need vacations, leisure time, quiet time, and reading. But these are not necessarily the contemplative journey, and sometimes they actually keep us from it by excessive self-analysis, the need to work it all out, or the desire to avoid people and problems. Introverts have no natural head start into contemplation. Their busyness and control needs just take a different shape from those of the extrovert.

It is important that we continue to clarify and hold to these two pivots of our lives. Rightly sought, action and contemplation will always regulate, balance, and convert each other. Separately, they are dead-ended and trapped in personality. The clear goal of our Center [for Action and Contemplation] is to meet people "where they are at" and help them trust "where they are not at." For all of us it is an endless rhythmic dance. The step changes now and then, but Someone Else always leads.

THE SYMBOL OF THE RISING SUN

When I worked with the Indians in New Mexico as a deacon, I remember this old Indian lady telling me a lovely story:

You know, our parents never really taught us about prayer. We didn't memorize prayers. But every morning, my mother would wake us up, and as little children we'd have to sit on the steps of our house facing east. And she'd say, "Be quiet. You have to be quiet while you sit here. You watch the sun come up." Me and my brothers and sisters would have to sit on the steps and watch the sun rise every morning. "As the sun comes," my mother would say to us, "welcome it. Welcome it to the world. And tell it, as it goes over the earth, it should drop its blessings on all people." That was our prayer every day.

You can claim that this was a pagan kind of a prayer, but today that woman is a contemplative who prays eight Rosaries a day. Where did her prayer life start? She didn't enroll in a course on contemplation; her mother taught her how to watch the rising sun and make it a prayer.

When I was preaching in Puerto Rico and told that story, it surprised me when some of the young boys asked if we could get up and watch the rising sun. Next morning, a group of us were sitting there watching the sunrise, and about half of them said they had never in their whole life seen the sun rise. There is something transcendent about it—maybe it is mythological, maybe nonrational, but somehow it is a symbol of God never giving up. If you can watch the event as God trying again, every morning putting the sun over this world, it can be a beautiful prayer experience.

EINSTEIN: THE NEW WAY OF KNOWING

As Einstein said, "No problem can be solved from the same level of consciousness that created it." I try to teach a contemplative stance toward life that gives people an entirely new way of knowing the world, and that has the power to move them beyond mere ideology and dualistic thinking.

What religion calls contemplation is the only mind that is broad enough and deep enough to answer the real and important questions. Mature religion will always lead you to some form of prayer, meditation, or contemplative mind to balance out our usually calculative mind. Such "seeing" gives you the capacity to be happy and happily alone, rooted elsewhere, comfortable with paradox and mystery, and largely immune to mass consciousness and its false promises. It is called wisdom seeing.

THÉRÈSE OF LISIEUX: HOW YOU DO ANYTHING IS HOW YOU DO EVERYTHING

Your practice must somehow include the problem. Prayer is not the avoiding of distractions, but precisely how you deal with distractions. Contemplation is not the avoidance of the problem, but a daily merging with the problem, and finding its full resolution. What you quickly and humbly learn in contemplation is that how you do anything is probably how you do everything. If you are brutal in your inner reaction to your own littleness and sinfulness, your social relationships and even your politics will probably be the same—brutal. One sees a woman overcome this split in an autobiography like St.

Thérèse of Lisieux's *Story of a Soul*. This young contemplative nun is daily dealing with her irritations, judgments, and desire to run from her fellow sisters in the convent. She faces her own mixed motives and pettiness. She is constant in her concern for those working actively in the missions. But her goal is always compassion and communion. She suffers her powerlessness until she can finally break through to love. She holds the tension within herself (the essence of contemplation) until she herself is the positive resolution of that tension.

A RIVER MEDITATION

Most of us have lived our whole lives with a steady stream of consciousness, with a continual flow of ideas, images, and feelings. And at every moment of our lives we cling to such ideas or feelings: I don't have the idea; the idea has me. I don't have a feeling; the feeling has me. We have to discover who this I really is, the one who has these feelings or these thoughts. Who are we ourselves—behind our thoughts and feelings?

I'm sure that most people in the Western world have never really met the person who they themselves really are. Because at every moment, all our life long, we identify ourselves either with our thoughts, our self-image, or our feelings. We have to find a way to get behind our thoughts, feelings, and self-image. We have to discover the face that we already had before we were born. We have to find out who we were all along in God before we did anything right or wrong. This is the first goal of contemplation.

I ask you to imagine a river or stream. You're sitting on the bank of this river, where boats and ships are sailing past. While the stream flows past your inner eye, I ask you to name each one of these vessels. For example, one of the boats could be called "my anxiety about tomorrow." Or along comes the ship "objections to my husband," or the boat "Oh, I don't do that well." Every judgment that you pass is one of those boats. Take the time to give each one of them a name, and then let it move on.

For some people this is a very difficult exercise, because we're used to jumping aboard the boats immediately. As soon as we own a boat, and identify with it, it picks up energy. But what we have to practice is un-possessing, letting go. With every idea, with every image that comes into our head we say, "No, I'm not that; I don't need that; that's not me." Again and again we have to tell ourselves this. Some of the boats that are accustomed to our jumping aboard them immediately think we just didn't see them the first time. That's why they head back upstream and return. The boat says, "But before this he always used to get mad at his wife. Why didn't he this time?" Some of you will feel the need to torpedo your boats. But don't attack them. Don't hate them or condemn them: this is also an exercise in nonviolence. You aren't allowed to hate your soul. The point is to recognize things and to say, "That's not necessary; I don't need that." But do it very amiably. If we learn to handle our own souls tenderly and lovingly, then we'll be able to carry this same loving wisdom into the world outside.

MEISTER ECKHART AND THE RECIPROCAL GAZE

God is Being itself, but also a Being that is more me than I am myself. This changes everything. God has become a Thou, and not just an energy field. And I have become an I, and not just a statistic. And the path is relationship itself and not just practice, discipline, or holy posture. Authentic contemplation of the Other, through all the necessary stages of personal relationship, calls us beyond our tiny and false selves and into The Self. We become the One we gaze upon. And "the eyes by which we look back at God are the same eyes by which God has first looked at us" (Meister Eckhart). This reciprocal gaze is the true self, perfectly given and always waiting to be perfectly received. It is so dear and so precious that it needs no external payoffs whatsoever. The true self is abundantly content.

TRY TO LOVE A STONE

Once upon a time, a small Jewish boy went to his rabbi and said he didn't know how to love God. "How can I love God when I've never seen him?" asked the boy. "I think I understand how to love my mother, my father, my brother, my little sister, and even the people in our neighborhood, but I don't know how I'm supposed to love God."

The rabbi looked at the little boy and said, "Start with a stone. Try to love a stone. Try to be present to the most simple and basic thing in reality so you can see its goodness and beauty. Then let that goodness and beauty come into you. Let it speak to you. Start with a stone." The boy nodded with understanding.

"Then, when you can love a stone," the rabbi continued, "try a flower. See if you can love a flower. See if you can be present to it and let its beauty come into you. See if you can let its life come into you and you can give yourself to it. You don't have to pluck it, possess it, or destroy it. You can just love it over there in the garden." The boy nodded again.

"I'm not saying it's wrong to pick flowers," added the rabbi. "I'm just asking you to learn something from the flower without putting it in a vase." The boy smiled, which meant he understood—or maybe he didn't. Just in case he didn't, the rabbi chose the boy's pet dog as the next object of loving and listening. The boy nodded and smiled when the rabbi talked about his dog; he even said, "Yes, Rabbi."

"Then," the rabbi went on, "try to love the sky and the mountains, the beauty of all creation. Try to be present to it in its many forms. Let it speak to you and let it come into you." The boy sensed the rabbi wanted to say some more, so he nodded again, as if he understood.

"Then," the rabbi said, "try to love a woman. Try to be faithful to a woman and sacrifice yourself for her. After you have loved a stone, a flower, your little dog, the mountain, the sky, and a woman, then you'll be ready to love God."

How lovely, and how true! Too many people have tried to short-circuit the process of learning to love God. Instead of starting with a stone and working their way up to God, they quickly pretend to have some immediate contact with divine revelation. I don't want to discourage anyone from running to God, but some people don't yet know how to run or how to love the stones. They don't yet know how to perceive, how to be faithful, how to sacrifice, how to see without trying to control. They probably try to control because, like the rest of us, they feel weak, alienated, and out of communion with reality. But control never works in the spiritual life. The "undergoing" (passion) teaches more than the fixing and explaining (action).

People with little or no patience for communing with stones, flowers, pets, or human beings will probably not have much more patience communing directly with God. . . . They will most likely distort the revelation of God and use it for their own purposes. The false, egocentric self, disconnected from union, will be unable to see things correctly or enjoy them for themselves. The fragmented person seems to fragment everything else. The reconnected person sees rightly and, not surprisingly, sees God, too.

IT'S ALL A MATTER OF SEEING

As soon as we distance ourselves from the control center of our brains, as soon as we free ourselves from the comfortable principles of our preconceived theology, as soon as we've gotten to the point where we know only that we actually know nothing, then the transcendent can reach us. Then we are no longer caught in the myth of reason, the myth of science. Then we open to the nonrational as well, to grace, to the transcendent, to the burning bush. It's all a matter of seeing.

WHAT REALLY IS

The best definition I know for contemplation is as follows: Contemplation is a long, loving look at what really is. The essential element in this experience is time. There is a qualitative difference between ten minutes and ten hours, and even more, of course, between ten hours and ten days. We have to find a place where we can receive all our experiences without repressing anything. We need a place where there's room to consider everything that we've done—and not done—in our life, a place that's bigger than Yes or No, a place bigger than the judgments that we pass. At this all-embracing place God becomes quite clear. Here there is room for every part of you and for God's presence.

THE FIRST STAGES OF CONTEMPLATIVE PRAYER

Unless we learn to let go of our feelings, we don't have the feelings; the feelings have us.

We have to ask: Who is the "I" that has these feelings? The spiritual journey leads us back to this "I." But most men and women in the West have never encountered it. Instead they've become identified with their stream of consciousness, with their feelings. I'm not saying that you should suppress and deny your feelings. I'm challenging you to name them, identify them, and observe them. But don't fight them and don't identify with them. Teaching this art is teaching contemplative prayer in its first stages.

Now you might ask: "What does this have to do with God? I thought prayer was supposed to be talking to God or searching for God. You seem to be saying that prayer is first of all about me and getting myself out of the way?" That is exactly what I am saying. God is already present. God's Spirit is dwelling within you. You cannot search for what you already have. You cannot talk God into "coming" into you by longer and more urgent prayers. All you can do is become quieter, smaller, and less filled with your own self and its flurry of ideas and feelings. Then God will be obvious in the very now of things.

RADICAL CONTEMPLATION

I am convinced that contemplation is the most radical thing that we can teach and live. What else will lead us beyond words, endless theories, and the prison of the private self? The first commandment of non-idolatry and the second of God as Holy Mystery are all that we can ever offer.

THE PERFECT REFLECTOR

The restored Job and the risen Christ are images of the substantial self, no longer private, separate, or autonomous, but hidden in God. The true self is not lost in a transitory house of mirrors, but founded in the unreflected and perfect Reflector we all long for. . . . All we need to know is that God is looking back—and not away from our gaze.

GOD IS CARRYING ME

Allowing God to be our Lord is not something we can do as easily as believing this, doing that, attending this, or avoiding that. It is always a process of a lifetime, a movement toward union that will always feel like a loss of self-importance and autonomy. The private ego will resist and rationalize in every way that it can. My experience is that, apart from suffering, failure, humiliation, and pain, none of us will naturally let go of our self-sufficiency. We will think that our story is just about us. It isn't. . . . My significance comes from who-I-am-in-God, who-I-am-as-part-of-a-much-larger-whole. I am somehow a representative of God, and God is carrying me, both the good and the bad parts.

CONTEMPLATIVE SURRENDER

Contemplation, in non-mystified language, is the ability to meet Reality in its most simple and direct form. When I let go of my judgments, my agenda, my tyrannical emotive life, my attachment to my positive or negative self-image, I am naked, poor, and ready for The Big Truths. Without some form of contemplative surrendering, I see little hope for breakthrough, for new ground, for moving beyond the hysterical ideologies of Left and Right, the small mind, and the clutching ego.

OUR INNER OBSERVER: FAIR WITNESS

We all play our games, cultivating our prejudices and our unredeemed vision of the world. That is why we must accept our gift in order to see our sin—and we must accept our sin in order to recognize how gifted we are. We have to limit our gift; otherwise our sin becomes a trap—while we call it virtue. This is traditional church teaching. Thomas Aquinas and many Scholastics said that all people choose something that appears good. No one willingly does evil. Each of us has put together a construct by which we explain why what we do is necessary and good. That is why it is so necessary to "discern the spirits" *(1 Cor. 12:10)*. We need support in unmasking our false self and in distancing ourselves from our illusions. For this it is necessary to install a kind of "inner observer." Some people talk about a "fair witness." At first that sounds impossible, but after a while it becomes quite natural. We're dealing with a part of ourselves that's honest—not only in the negative sense, but in the positive, too. It tells us, for example, "You really love God and long for God. You are good. Stop butchering yourself so brutally. You are a daughter or son of God. You can feel compassion." This helps us to distinguish moralizing from real morality, guilty feelings from real guilt, false pride from genuine strength.

DIFFERENT FORMS OF PRAYER

People have different temperaments and different rhythms, and you have to discover how to pray according to your own rhythm and temperament.

I find many people very dissatisfied because of their unusual prayer lives. They feel they are not doing it as they should. For some, perhaps, Tuesday afternoon from one o'clock to five is going to be their prayer time because during this particular time slot they can slow down, take off, and drive to the country (or whatever it might be). For others, it is absolutely important to start every day with prayer. They don't feel right all day if they don't get up early and spend half an hour in prayer. For some, prayer time is after supper; for others, it's after their kids are asleep or before they get out of bed in the morning. Still others take two days a month for retreat to saturate themselves with prayer. That of course doesn't mean they're not seeking communion with the Lord throughout the week.

There is no need to feel guilty about when, how, and how often you formally pray. As you come to understand your own temperament, you will understand your way to pray. Those of us whose minds are always racing might need the Jesus Beads or the Rosary. . . . All repetition "leaves the mind barren" *(1 Cor. 14:15)* and thereby open to "another mind." . . . "Doers," however, need liturgical prayer, where we can kneel, stand, sit, move around, eat, drink, and shake hands. Walking meditation, for example, took the form of processions or the Stations of the Cross.

Those who are primarily "be-ers" may need a prayer of quiet. We may need charismatic and contemplative prayer forms that move beyond images. Or we may need prayer that employs our fantasy, imagination, and memory. Those three faculties have been neglected in our spirituality tradition. In much Christian meditation, we tend to emphasize the faculties of our mind, exercising the memory, intellect, and will. Often we read our prayers from a printed page, which is fine for liturgical assemblies as long as it does not become an avoidance of spontaneous prayer from the heart. In the course of our lives, we will likely move between these different prayer forms at different stages of our journey.

CRAWLING UP ON THE CLOUD

Eternal life is not something sought after—it is something responded to. That means it's a gift. We don't have to fight for it. We don't have to work hard to earn it. We don't have to obey laws in order to deserve it. We already have it. Love knows this.

When St. Thérèse of Lisieux, the Little Flower, was caught up in her little embarrassing and painful moments of the day and her emotions were taking over, she was not free to be present to that moment because she was hurting so much. She explained, "At times like that, what I do is try to get God's perspective. I figure God sees everything—the beginning, middle, and end of my life. I imagine he's sitting up on a cloud, looking down on the whole of my life, so I try to crawl up on that cloud. Once I get up there and look down on my whole life, I don't take this moment too seriously. Then I don't get trapped by it."

Ironically, the freedom to live in the present requires that you be free from the present. To truly give yourself to right now, today, you have to embrace the vision of your whole lifetime—time and eternity. Crawl up on Therese's cloud . . . so that you're not trapped, enslaved, and controlled by the present moment. On the other side, when you know that everything is important, then no-thing really matters and you can let go. The big story frees you from the tyranny of me and now. Your identity is from God, and you enjoy the divine perspective. One person's lack of recognition of you or criticism of you is not going to destroy you—because you are named by God. That is the religious reference point that simultaneously grounds you and frees you. It is the only way out of the revolving hall of mirrors.

MAKING A PLACE FOR CHRIST

On the way to contemplation we do the same thing that Jesus Christ did in the wilderness. Jesus teaches us not to say, "Lord, Lord," but to do the will of his Father. What must primarily concern us is that we do what Jesus has bidden us do. Jesus went into the wilderness, ate nothing for forty days, and made himself empty. Another image of that emptiness is the body of Mary. She can receive Jesus into that emptiness and bear Christ to the world because she is his poor handmaid.

Of course, emptiness in and of itself isn't enough. The point of emptiness is to get ourselves out of the way so that Christ can fill us up. As soon as we're empty, there's a place for Christ, because only then are we in any sense ready to recognize and accept Christ as the totally other, who is not me.

CONCEIVING CHRIST

The Incarnation had nothing to do with theology. It was rather about vulnerability, about letting go, about emptiness, about self-surrender—and none of that is in the head. It was a woman who said yes, so that Jesus could come into the world. And the more the Church gets out of its head and into its feminine soul, the more, I believe, it will become able to conceive Christ and carry him to term for the world. Not a Christ to fight over as Catholics or Protestants, as liberals or conservatives, but simply a Christ we can meet, a Christ we can stumble on, a Christ who won't let people "know" him, only love him.

CALLED TO A DEEPER PLACE

What we need is not excessive self-consciousness but authentic contemplation. When we discover ourselves "hidden with Christ in God," we don't need any kind of self-image at all. I hope this doesn't sound too esoteric, because it isn't; it's what happens in true prayer. This is what will happen when we expose ourselves to silence and stop exposing ourselves to the judgments of the world, when we stop continuously "picking up" the energy of others, when we stop thinking about what others think of us and what they take us to be. We are who we are in God—no more and no less.

That's why I have to go into the wilderness, where I let God call me by name to a deeper place. This is the peace that the world can't give. But I promise you that it's also the peace that the world can no longer take from you. This peace doesn't come about because of anything we do right. We have to discover what we have always been in God. When we get to this place, we will know and love ourselves, in spite of all the negative and opposing evidence. It is the spacious place of the soul. To live there is finally to be at home. This first and final home we carry with us all our lives. God is also at home there, and when we return we will have discovered simplicity.

FAITH WITHOUT FEELINGS

God often comes into this world quite unexpectedly, uninvited, and even unwanted. Take the charisms, for example—the many spiritual gifts of healing, tongues, and forgiveness; through them we experience the immediate action of God in this world. They're necessary for us to develop a taste for the holy. It's very sad that in Western Christianity so few people have a genuine sense of the sacred or an authentic access to it, the feeling that "I'd just like to kneel down." Without this, religion very quickly becomes sterile and rigid.

But on the other hand we can't strive first for transcendental or emotional experiences of faith, because if we do they can easily become a cheap substitute for real faith. Faith is ultimately faith, which means to believe and to know—without experience and without feelings. We might have to spend a whole lifetime walking in darkness, recalling the little we've experienced in the light.

WHAT'S HAPPENING IN HEAVEN

The most simple rule for discovering what we are to do on earth is to ask what's happening in heaven. What's happening in the heavenly kingdom is communion, unity, family. "Lord, your will be done on earth as it is happening in heaven." What God's love creates in heaven is perfect union. Union and communion are the goal of what God is doing on earth. God is not creating religion and righteousness—God is creating unity. That's why Jesus' basic rules for the kingdom are about forgiveness, reconciliation, healing, and communication. Those who are capable of union and communion are capable of God.

MOTHER TERESA: LIVING WITHOUT SECURITY

I spent three days immersed in the life, spirit, and ministries of Mother Teresa's community—the Missionaries of Charity—exactly a year after her death. The major sessions took place right next to her tomb, or in the large chapel immediately above. We ended on October 1, the feast of her patron, St. Thérèse. All the four hundred–plus local candidates, novices, and professed return for this day. The brothers and many of the lay volunteers also joined us for a full day of teaching, praying, and celebrating in the manner of the poor. It is probably the closest I will ever get to what those first idyllic days must have been like for the early Franciscans: utter joy in Jesus and his Gospel, poverty that is almost embarrassing but beautiful, unquestioned belief in what your life means and in what you are doing.

The sisters were not people needing security, answers, and order, as we see in most traditionalist movements in the West, but in fact people who were willing to live without security, with very few answers to their questions of mind and heart, and amid almost total disorder. All in union—hour by hour—with God ... Is this not the ultimate nonviolent life that we are searching for? In Mother Teresa's community the only "violence" seems to be toward the self—and not toward anybody else. In other words, I let God change me instead of first trying to change others. This is radical reform. Mother Teresa neither played the victim nor created victims, but like Jesus, she became the free and forgiving victim who carried the two sides of humanity inside of herself—until it transformed her and made her useable for God. I know of no other way out of our present and universal dilemma. Yet it has been the Gospel since the beginning.

FALLING IN LOVE WITH GOD

Some are convinced God is playing a game with them. When we experience God playing a game with us, we instinctively play another game, which is called religion. "How long,

O Lord?" is our attitude. "How long do we have to put up with this?" This pattern never seems to change until we encounter intimate love. . . .

But the good news is that we are still producing mystics. People are always falling in love with God, especially after they recognize that God loved them when they were unlovable, God trusted them when they could not trust themselves, and God forgave them when no one else would.

BELONGING TO GOD

It is much easier to belong to a group than to belong to God. To belong to a group one usually has to be convinced the group is "right"; to belong to God, one always knows one is as wrong as everybody else.

GOD IS A VERB OR BEING KNOWN THROUGH

"Everything exposed to the light itself becomes light," says Ephesians 5:14. In prayer, we merely keep returning the divine gaze and we become its reflection, almost in spite of ourselves *(2 Cor. 3:18)*. The word "prayer" has often been trivialized by making it into a way of getting what you want. I use "prayer" as the umbrella word for any interior journeys or practices that allow you to experience faith, hope, and love within yourself. It is not a technique for getting things, a pious exercise that somehow makes God happy, or a requirement for entry into heaven. It is much more like practicing heaven now.

The essential religious experience is that you are being "known through" more than knowing anything in particular yourself. Yet despite this difference, it can feel like true knowing. We can interchangeably call this new way of knowing contemplation, nondualistic thinking, or "third-eye" seeing. Such prayer, such seeing takes away your anxiety about figuring it all out fully for yourself, or needing to be right about your formulations. At this point, God becomes more a verb than a noun, more a process than a conclusion, more an experience than a dogma, more a personal relationship than an idea. There is Someone dancing with you, and you are not afraid of making mistakes.

IDENTIFYING WITH THE BELOVED

What we experience when we identify with the beloved—this is the achievement of the saints and mystics—is not "I love you by choice or devotion" but "I am you." That's the identification that happens on the spiritual journey. As Jesus put it, "I and the Father are one."

The object of devotion is not even out there anymore; it has been so taken in that I am over there, and the "over there" is in here.

HOW THE MYSTICS KNOW GOD

God, it seems, cannot really be known, but only related to. Or, as the mystics would assert, we know God by loving God, by trusting God, by placing our hope in God. It is a nonpossessive, nonobjectified way of knowing. It is always I-thou and never I-it, to use Martin Buber's wonderfully insightful phrases. God allows us to know him only by loving him. God, in that sense, cannot be "thought."

Part Six
TO DISCOVER THE TRUTH,
YOU MUST BECOME THE TRUTH

TRUTH IS A PERSON

Truth is finally a person and an encounter—much more than a concept that can be argued. We are realigned with truth when the real person meets the real God—which is exactly the stuff of spirituality, theology, and conversion.

HEARING THE DEEPER VOICE

How do we try to hear the Deeper Voice? When God speaks, it is first of all profoundly consoling and, as a result, demanding! Anybody who has walked long with God knows this. There are two utterly different forms of religion: one believes that God will love me if I change; the other believes that God loves me so that I can change! The first is the most common; the second follows upon an experience of personal Indwelling and personal love. Ideas inform us, but love forms us—in an intrinsic and lasting way. God is always willing to wait for the lasting transformations brought about by love.

THE FRUITS OF THE SPIRIT

When people submit to the gifts of God, when people open up to the charisma of God, God is faithful to those gifts. God maintains those gifts and allows people to keep using them. But that is not necessarily holiness. Gifts—even healing itself—are not a sign or proof of holiness. Rejoice not in displays of power, but only in expressions of union "that your names are written in heaven" *(Luke 10:20)*. The fruits of the Spirit are the only true signs of holiness. . . . Just because people do powerful things does not justify everything else they're doing. . . . Look instead for "love, joy, peace, patience, kindness, generosity, faithfulness, gentleness, and self-control" *(Gal. 5:22)*. This discernment of the presence of the Spirit will never be wrong.

THE GIFT OF INNER AUTHORITY

The Spirit confers the gift of inner authority. Only people of inner authority . . . will use the outer authority correctly. Otherwise, people use external authority as an excuse not to walk the inner journey and discover their own souls. The church is filled with people who are living on hearsay, who stand on someone else's authority, but do not know what they themselves know. There is no "I" there to believe in God.

Whom have you met? Whom are you speaking for? What do you think? What have you experienced as the truth? What is goodness? What is evil? What is life? What is justice? What is injustice? "Well, so-and-so says this, another author says that." But what do you say? As Jesus said to Peter, "Who

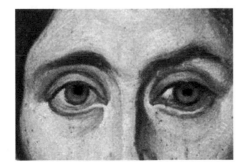

do you say I am?" *(Matt. 16:15)*. Note that he took him into foreign territory, outside his usual mirrors, to ask him this personal question. We probably need to start with a reliance upon expertise, tradition, and the elders (rebelliousness gets us nowhere either), but eventually God calls us into this kind of daring self-trust and self-risk that we see in Job.

"TO DWELL INSIDE OF THINGS"

According to the chemist-turned-philosopher Michael Polanyi, all knowing of truth can happen only inside a previous "tacit knowing" that is silent, unconscious, and unspoken—even to us. Text is always untrue or at least incomplete outside of context. He subverted all claims to perfect objectivity in science, philosophy, and religion. He never denied objective reality; he just said we must be humble and tentative about our ability to know it. We are all partial knowers; all verbalizations are filled with biography, preference, genius, and past hurts. We are always invested in our knowing. We are all wading in Heraclitus's ever-moving stream. This leads us to a necessary humility and to a very unsettling sense of the certitude that we all want and need. It seems we must somehow "kneel" to hear and see correctly. Polanyi said to his fellow scientists that the great geniuses had something more than detached, cold objectivity. They also had an ability "to dwell inside of things" that was more art than science, more poetry than prose, more spirit than rational control of the data. And more letting go than holding on.

Interestingly enough, this hard-core scientist taught an almost spiritual method that he called "indwelling" in order to get closer to truth. Geniuses, saints, inventors, discoverers, prophets, all truly creative people somehow have the "feel" for their area of giftedness. And it is almost impossible for them to know how they get that "feel." That's why they themselves know it is a gift (or in church language, a charism). We all know that some people say all the right words, but they still don't have it. Yet what is "it"? Somehow you can be a scientist but not an artist. You can be a perfect technician but create nothing. You can be a functionary wearing the uniform, but the something that makes life happen is not there. We all know you can be a priest or bishop without having led a single person to God.

. . . Polanyi concluded that it was necessary to "tune in" with intense personal involvement and even love of the situation and the other to be able to hear and see the situation truthfully. He said all truthful knowing had to acknowledge a tacit knowing (which is what religion means by faith, according to Polanyi), and this tacit knowing has something to do with trusting it, allowing it, believing in it, and not starting with fear, suspicion, rejection. In other words, only those who love rightly see rightly! Only those who are situated correctly in the correct universe can read the situation with freedom and grandeur. Text plus full context equals genius. Only the true believer can trust that larger context, even to the point of including God. Then the believer is at a cosmic level of peacefulness: reality is good, the world is coherent, it is all going somewhere. That allows the believer to move ahead without a rejecting or superior attitude.

Only those who love rightly see rightly!

Such people are constantly learning and always teachable and will likely do good things—this is, I am sure, a secular name for faith. Eric Hoffer, the street philosopher, put it this way: "In times of great change [which is always], learners inherit the earth, while the learned find themselves beautifully equipped for a world that no longer exists." Faith itself, like the discernment of spirits, is actually a way to keep us learning, growing, and being transformed into God—not just a security blanket of doctrinal statements and moral principles.

AN INVITATION TO LIVE WITH HIM

Here is how Jesus teaches the disciples—his seminary, his lifestyle. He takes them with him, and watching him, they learn the cycle and the rhythm of his life. He doesn't teach them merely conceptual information as we were taught in our seminary. He introduces them to a lifestyle. The only way he can do that is to invite them to live with him.

"But the crowds got to know where he had gone and they went after him. He made them welcome and he talked to them about the kingdom of God and he cured those who were in need of healing" *(Luke 9:11)*. Can't you just see the apostles standing at Jesus' side, watching him, noticing how he does things: how he talks to people, how he waits, how he listens, how he's patient, how he depends upon his Father, how he takes time for prayer, how he doesn't respond cynically or bitterly but trustfully and yet truthfully?

The whole New Testament—all the Christian Scriptures together—maintains a beautiful balance between immanence and transcendence. God is totally beyond us, yet in Jesus God is also among us and within us—a creative tension that needs to be maintained both in experience and in theology.

THE DISCERNMENT OF SPIRITS

Our goal consists in doing the will of the Father in heaven. Thus we first have to remove our attachment to our own will, so that we can recognize the difference between the two. Throughout history, many people who did horrible things were unshakably convinced that they were doing the will of God. That's why we have to find an instrument to distinguish between God and us. Paul calls this the gift of discernment of spirits. We have to learn when our own spirit is at work and when the Spirit of God is at work.

WE ARE CO-CREATORS

Action does not mean activism, busyness, or do-goodism. Action, however, does mean a decisive commitment toward involvement and engagement in the social order. Issues will not be resolved by mere reflection, discussion, or even prayer. God "works together with" *(Rom. 8:28)* all those who love. To requote so many saints, "We must work as if it all depends on us and pray as if it all depends on God." That does not imply frenetic programming, but it does say that our work is essential and even cocreative of the new world. Our action is apparently important and dignified in God's eyes. In a real sense we even have a bias toward action, because there is no reason to believe that God gives us anything that we have not said yes to by work, decision, and effort.

JESUS' AUTHORITY

Jesus says nothing to us that he hasn't heard first. He teaches only what has been told to him, only what has been taught to him by the Father. He is, first, a faithful son; out of that sonship experience comes the power to be the father that creates this spiritual family, the church. . . . To be a brother and a son, you have to let yourself be loved. You have to know how to receive love.

SALUS: INNER CLARITY

Salvation (*salus:* healing) is not dependent on feeling or any person's response to me. It is not a theory believed, a theology proclaimed, or a group that gives one identity. It is an inner clarity that forever allows one to recognize bogus authority and pseudo-surrender. This salvation cannot be acquired by a simple process of self-examination, new insight, or ego-possession. It is a gift received when the will has given up control and we are standing in that threshold place which allows us to see anew.

LEARNING HOW TO BE TAUGHT

For Jesus, "discipleship" is another word for sonship and daughterhood. Those who cannot be sons cannot be brothers and, finally, cannot be fathers. Those who cannot be daughters cannot be sisters and, finally, cannot be mothers. Disciples must follow that sequence. This involves learning first how to be sons and daughters, learning how to be taught, how to receive love, how to be loved, how to be taken care of, how to be believed in.

But a proud and rebellious people do not like to be sons and daughters; they immediately want to be fathers and mothers—that is, they want power, they want to be in charge. Therefore, be careful of any fatherhood in the church that does not come out of primary sonship. And do not trust any fatherhood in the church that does not come out of practical brotherhood. It will have little true authority.

This is what religious orders were initially trying to do: provide settings in which we could learn to be sons and brothers, or daughters and sisters, before we attempted to be spiritual fathers and mothers. Calling each other "Brother" or "Sister," monks and nuns were supposed to have spiritual guides and directors and live under their care—learning how to be taught, how to receive love, how to be healed and transformed—before they would dare to father or mother others.

So Jesus, first of all, steps into his ministry as son, not as a father. Rather he lets the Father teach him. Because Jesus is always listening to the Father, the Father is continually teaching him, and his growth continues.

For example, you know that beautiful and powerful expression, "Amen, Amen" that was always used at the end of a prayer in Judaism? Jesus puts it at the beginning of everything important he says. Why would Jesus do that, since as a good Jew he knows the expression belongs at the end? What that probably means ... is that Jesus is saying that he has already heard in his heart what the Father wants him to say. So when Jesus is saying "Amen, Amen," he is affirming what he has just heard interiorly from the Father. He then passes it on to us.

FIRST I HAVE TO ACT: THE MYSTERIOUS WISDOM OF FAITH

First I have to act, and then I'll understand—meaning the whole person will understand. Then I'll know what I know. But I really won't know why I know. I also won't be able to prove to you why I know something; it's the mysterious wisdom of faith. It's the wisdom you learn only when you're on the way. This is a lesson nobody else can teach you, neither the pope nor biblical authorities; you have to go down this road yourself. That's what the "primacy of action" means. Persist at that deeper place in yourself where the "both-and" is located. This is the place of the soul, the place of wisdom, toward which we have to move. Don't be afraid! Fear comes from a need to control. And we are not in control anyway.

NAMED BY GOD

Happiness is finally an inside job. We are too often "reeds swaying in the breeze" *(Matt. 11:7)*, dependent moment by moment on others' reaction and approval. This is the modern self: insubstantial, whimsical, totally dependent and calling itself "free."

I have worked with people in whom I have seen this change: Once they were responding primarily to life outside themselves, but through contact with what I will call

"authentic transcendence," they're drawing their life from within. They're not letting other people name them. They are named by God, and they have recognized that name as their deepest and truest self.

LARGER THAN LIFE

Our greatest strength [as Catholics] is to be true traditionalists, to go all the way with the tradition and find the entire pattern. The whole broad, deep, rich pattern. True Catholicism should be *kata holon*: according to the whole. The essential charism of the Catholic Church is precisely catholicity, even if we don't always achieve it.

"Catholic" could be translated as "universalist." Our word today is "holistic." This means the whole picture, not just one century or one cultural experience. What is God saying to the whole of humanity? Catholicity is still, along with our positive anthropology, the greatest strength of the Catholic Church: We have the possibility of drawing from all the sciences, countries, and centuries, and putting all that wisdom together. For all our neuroses about control and the body, Catholicism is still the most successful multicultural institution on the earth.

When we meet a true Catholic, we meet a person who is both grounded and inclusive. We do not meet a lot of them—most so-called Catholics are not catholic; they're ethnic, or they're provincial, or merely American. True Catholics have moved beyond their cultural prejudices. They include all the ages, not just the present century. They put all the accumulated wisdom together, and they emerge as extraordinary people.

People such as Thomas Merton or Dorothy Day or Mother Teresa are larger than life. They come out of this enormously deep Catholic tradition. They are always universal people. You cannot identify them with any one country or culture.

JESUS' JOURNEY AND OURS

We know from our own experience that it is not enough to know interiorly who we are—we need confirmation of the fact from others. Identity is a social construct, too. We ask others how they see us. Jesus does the same. For example, he asks Peter the disciple, "Who do people say that I am?" He asks, "What am I for you?" *(See Luke 9:18–21.)*

The way we all come to know who we are happens, in great part, through other people telling us who we are. We learn elements of our identity in the ways they relate and react to us. And we never seem to stop inquiring about ourselves.

Throughout his life on this planet, Jesus' self-knowledge continues to grow. I don't know any contemporary biblical scholars who would dare to say, "It was at this point or that point in his life when Jesus fully realized who he was." Some suggest it was at his baptism. Others say his self-knowledge remained a continuously rising consciousness during his life. Others claim it was not until his resurrection itself that Jesus fully knew his identity and nature. Paul in Romans 1:3–4 could be interpreted that way. Perhaps not until the resurrection did the human consciousness of Jesus come to understand what we would later call him in Nicene theology: the Son of God and the Second Person of the Blessed Trinity.

When you approach the Gospels this way—with Jesus continuing to grow and develop in self-understanding—you'll find that they become much more real and alive for you. The stories will become more identifiable and transferable to other persons and situations. Jesus will become a real model and mentor of the process of faith itself instead of just the object of our faith. We believe "in him, through him, and with him," as the Eucharistic Prayer says.

Luke tells us that Jesus walked the journey of faith just as you and I do. That's the compelling message of the various dramas where Jesus needed faith—during his temptation in the desert, during his debates with his adversaries, in the garden, and on the cross. We like to imagine that Jesus did not flinch, did not doubt, did not ever question his Father's love. The much greater message is that in his humanity he did flinch, did ask questions, did have doubts—and still remained faithful.

SOMETHING NEW: HOLY FOOLS

Those who will lead into the future will have some hard-won virtues that I will try to describe here. But there is one character type that we cannot do without. Those who name and exemplify what God is doing will be "holy fools."

107

By the holy fool I mean what the Bible and mythic literature have always presented as the "savior." They are persons who are happily, but not naively, innocent of everything that the rest of us take for granted. They alone can trust and live the new work of God because they are not protecting the past by control (conservatives) or reacting against the past by fixing (liberals). Both of these are too invested in their own understanding to let go and let God do something new on earth:

> Bring forward the people that is blind, yet has eyes,
> that is deaf and yet has ears. . . .
> No need to recall the past,
> No need to think about what was done before.
> See, I am doing something new!
> Even now before it comes to light, can you not see it?
>
> —*Isaiah 43:8, 18–19 (written in exile)*

According to pattern, the wise fools are always formed in the testing ground of exile when the customary and familiar are taken away and they must go much deeper and much higher for wisdom. As a result, they no longer fit or belong among their own. Yet they alone can point the way to the ever new Jerusalem. Conventional wisdom is inadequate, even if widely held by good people. Thus it is only Parsifal, the "perfect fool," who can find the path to the Holy Grail.

It is Paul, isolated but enthralled by a vision of universal Gospel, who can say,

> Make no mistake about it: if you think you are wise,
> in the ordinary sense of the word, then you must
> learn to be a fool before you can really be wise.
>
> —*1 Corinthians 3:18*

... The holy fool is the last stage of the wisdom journey. It is the man or woman who knows his or her dignity and therefore does not have to polish or protect it. It is the man or woman who has true authority and does not have to defend it or anyone else's authority. It is the child of God who has met the One who "hurls galaxies and watches over sparrows" (Greg Flannery) and therefore can comfortably be a child of God. These, and these alone, can be trusted to proclaim the Reign of God.

IBN AL-ARABI: BECOMING TRANSPARENT

The only thing that the silence has taught me: our lives are useable for God. We need not be effective, but only transparent and vulnerable. God takes it all from there, and there is not much point in comparing who is better, right, higher or lower, or supposedly saved. We are all partial images slowly coming into focus, to the degree we allow and filter the Light and Love of God.

Let me end with a quote from a Muslim mystic that I discovered while in hermitage. There it delighted me for days on end, yet now, back in the flurry of images and emotions, I block this simple Light and this always sweet sadness: "God sighs to become known in us. God is delivered from solitude by the people in whom God reveals himself. The sorrow of the unknown God is softened through and in us" *(Ibn al-Arabi, 1165–1240).*

That's enough work for all of our remaining years. All we can be is transparent and vulnerable. Our authority will be the authority of those who have passed through—and come out on the other side—dead and alive.

Part Seven
WHEN YOU ARE TRANSFORMED,
OTHERS WILL BE TRANSFORMED THROUGH YOU

"DANGEROUSLY FREE":
COMPASSION FROM CONTEMPLATION

The purpose of letting go is to freely lay hold of something. And the purpose of this new liberation from bondage is to commit ourselves from free and healthy motives. The effect of contemplation is authentic action, and if contemplation doesn't lead to genuine action, then it remains only self-preoccupation.

But I'm convinced that if you stick with it, if you do this regularly, then you will come to the inner place of compassion. In this place you'll notice how much the suffering of the world is your suffering, and how committed you are to this world, not cerebrally, but from the much deeper perspective of your soul. At this inner place of compassion you're indestructible, because there you find the peace that the world cannot give. You don't need to win anymore; you just need to do what you have to do, as simplistic and naive as that might sound. That's why Augustine could make such an outrageous statement as "love God and do what you want"! People who are living from a truly God-centered place instead of a self-centered place are dangerously free precisely because they are tethered at the center.

PLATO'S HOLY MADNESS

The "holy madness" that Plato described as love makes control unnecessary, unattractive, and unreal. Once you have enjoyed real power, mere control is a counterfeit and a nuisance. People of power empower those around them. Controlling people control those around them. Which do you want to be? Which do you want to do?

"LOVE MUST BE BROUGHT TO EARTH"

Power and love are not mutually exclusive, but until I unlearn power in its usual form (and it is indeed an unlearning, which Christianity calls conversion), the mysterious event of love will not happen. If love does happen—a mystery, God-like—that we "fall" into and sometimes decide for, power emerges in a whole new form. This power is not only good but necessary and the conjugal partner of love.... Love must be brought to earth; power must be lifted to the liberating heavens. Love relationships are necessary to make life bearable and beautiful; power relationships are necessary to get anything done.

What most people call power is just control. When I need to see that actions are done my way, I might have control over passing events, but that is not power in any full sense. Real persons of power can act, succeed, thrive—even when they do not have control. Power is the ability to act from the fullness of who I am, the capacity to establish and maintain a relationship with people and things, and the freedom to give myself away. If that sounds like religion's definition of a saint, you are right. Saints are the discoverers of that ideal blend between love and power.

THE CHRIST MOSAIC

Jesus Christ is our truth. That truth was and continues to be communicated to the church in its entirety for the benefit of the church in its entirety. That whole-church perspective should provide a good antidote for any pride and conceit any of us might have, since none of us in our finite minds and experience can begin to comprehend the whole Christ or even the whole church. Each of us is one little piece of the grand Christ mosaic, and we rejoice in that and give ourselves to it. But it is important to remain conscious that we are only one little part of the whole. As long as we stay in that consciousness, we will continue to remain available to the truth as it comes to us.

THE GOSPEL CALLS US TO COMMUNITY

The Gospel calls the whole world to a kind of community, to the possibility of a life that can be shared. But community is an art form, and there are obviously many possible ways of coming together. I know many religious who live in monasteries but who don't have the capacity for community life:

they're too imprisoned in themselves. And at the same time I know many nuns who live alone in apartments but are totally community-oriented, bound up and interconnected with the lives of many people. The secret lies in the way you let other people get through to you, and the way you move out of yourself. This is, of course, at once the mystery of spirituality and the mystery of vulnerability and powerlessness.

When a person is on a serious inner journey to his or her own powerlessness and is also in immediate contact with the powerless men and women of the world, then community will result.

If one of the two is lacking, people won't be community-oriented. Without an interior life and what we call "love of justice," most communities just serve themselves. We have to look out for this particularly in the United States, because we're by nature rather narcissistic. Because so many families break up, many people naturally enter communities to experience there the family they never had. That's understandable, but I'm convinced that people also have to be called to a vision outside themselves. Up to a certain point, even if not totally, we become healed and liberated despite ourselves—as a by-product. We can't spend our whole life working primarily to heal ourselves, because that comes by grace—it's a gift. This doesn't mean that we shouldn't take the time to work at our problems, but I believe the therapeutic society has its limits.

COMMUNITY: IDEAL AND REAL

Around the beginning of the 1970s I was very busy with the "community of communities" (a network of American base communities). Whenever I talk about this with Jim

Wallis, one of the founder/pastors of the Sojourners community and magazine, we wonder why so many communities started up and then folded.

... I think they had a hard time integrating spirituality and commitment with social justice issues. Some of them developed too much into "therapeutic communities" and imploded. After two or three years many members asked themselves, "What am I still doing here?" Many of the once politically oriented communities attracted a crowd of idealists, and then wore each other out with their idealism. Often they were more in love with their own ideals than with reality. If people haven't gone on a serious spiritual journey it's easy to predict that they'll be more in love with the idea of community than with the real thing.

I keep saying to new groups that it's very important to be extremely honest from the beginning about the real expectations and presuppositions that you bring with you.

SACRIFICE IS GIVING OURSELVES TO THE OTHER

Sacrifice comes from the words *sacrum facere*—to make sacred or holy. We make something holy by reconnecting it to the whole—in our case specifically by giving ourselves away to the other. A sacrifice does not mean that God is pleased by pain. It is, rather, a consecration by the self for the other, an offering of the self for the other. That, for some reason, is always convincing to human nature. When we go beyond the call of duty, when we lay our life down for our brother or sister, those for whom we make such a sacrifice are able to believe our love and believe that they can do the same. Thus redemptive suffering always generates immense life in others.

WE SHOULD BE THE LEAVEN

Jesus invites us as the Church to become a new community of human beings; he calls us a little flock. I don't believe he ever wanted us to be the whole—only the part. He said we should be the yeast, the leaven, not the whole loaf. He called us to be the salt, but we want to be the whole meal. He urged us to be the light that illumines the mountaintop, but we want to be the whole mountain. The images that Jesus uses are very modest and yet very strong. . . . It's very difficult now for us to be merely leaven and salt and light. We hardly know how to do that. We want to lead; we want the way of power. We thought we had to be the whole loaf, whereas he tells us to be just the leaven. That is a much more humble, fragile, and even invisible position. It feels powerless and will appeal only to people who don't need power.

SAINTS: CHANNELING GOD'S POWER

To those who call upon God in faith, to those who trust in God, God's power can be channeled through their lives to

bring good into the world: to heal, change, and transform events and people. But where saints are not present, where people who are open to God are unavailable, there is no clear channel of God's presence in the world. Nature, changes of times, and sinners largely direct the course of this world. But the leaven of saints, the "ten just men," are enough to keep the world from self-destruction.

YOU ARE AN INSTRUMENT

We seem to operate in an archetypal way for one another, quite apart from our actual personality. I remember how inauthentic I felt when I first raised my right hand as a twenty-seven-year-old new priest to bless a packed church; many of those in attendance were older than myself. Only later did I realize what words I was using. I was not speaking in my own name, but "in the name of the Father and of the Son." I was not blessing them. I had no power of my own with which to empower them, not at age twenty-seven, but I was somehow a channel. . . . Religious transformation works best when you know you are an instrument and not the origin, an aqueduct and not the source.

SPEAKING A WORD THAT IS TRUTH

God has to call us out of our need to control, to change, to convert other people. We are not called to control, change, and convert other people. We're simply called to be present to them and to be Jesus to them: to be present to them as he would be present to them. He takes it from there. If he wants to convert, control, or challenge them, then that's the Spirit's work. Our job, as was his in his earthly life, is to come into

the world, to be present, and to speak a word that is truth-
and life-giving. Then it is all up to God.

The most a preacher does is entice you, attract you, and
call you out of yourself to live a new kind of life. But the
Gospel cannot happen in your head alone. As I am fond of
repeating, you never think yourself into a new way of living.
You invariably live yourself into a new way of thinking.

TRUTH AND HUMILITY

The nondual/contemplative mind holds truth humbly,
knowing that if it is true, it is its own best argument, and
any formulation is still partial and "imperfect," as Paul says
in I Corinthians 13:12. The contemplative knows that truth
held arrogantly will not bear the wonderful fruit of truth.
Moral outrage at the ideas of others hardly ever serves God's
purposes, only our own. Non-polarity thinking teaches you
how to hold creative tensions, how to live with paradox and
contradictions, how to not run from mystery, and therefore
how to actually practice what all religions teach as necessary:

compassion, mercy, loving-kindness, patience, forgiveness, and humility.

GOD'S FIRST LIBERATION

Certain missionaries give out bread instead of the word of God. They give out bread in an attempt to solve their own problems. Perhaps they feel guilty. Perhaps they have a need to feel effective. Perhaps they doubt that they have anything to give in Christ. Perhaps they don't know that they have anything to give in praying with a person and giving a person hope or love. It actually is far easier to give a person a five-dollar bill than it is to share your faith with that person. It actually is easier to feed a person a meal than it is to let that person see your life at a deeper level.

Sometimes we should feed people or give a person a five-dollar bill. But don't use that as an excuse. Don't avoid the immediate power of God's first liberation, the liberation of the self.

SALVATION HAPPENS IN RELATIONSHIP

The Gospel happens between two or more people. Unless there is some place on this earth where it's happening between you and another person, I don't believe you have any criterion to judge whether it's happening at all. Unless you're in right relationship with at least one other person on this earth, unless there is some place you can give and receive love, I don't think you have any reason to think you're "saved." Salvation is not as antiseptic, unreal, and sterile as we've made it. Just because I like to read the Bible and go to church services, [I might think] "I'm saved." Is there at least one place in your life where you are giving and receiving love? If it happens in

one place, it can happen everywhere. If you are truly capable of loving one person, you're capable of loving more than one, eventually even your enemy, and finally, all.

The converse is also true. Unless you are capable of loving in general, you can't love just one. That's an important realization for young people, because they start dating at sixteen or seventeen and get totally enthralled with this one other person. Observe a contemporary dating syndrome: They dress up and look their best, neat and cool, for one other person, but all the rest of the week they're down on everyone else. Negative, cynical, bitter to everyone else, but to their sweetheart they are positive, hopeful, and delighted. "Oh, I love you. You're so sweet and good." Unless you love in general, you can't truly love in particular. And until you love in particular, you don't know how to love in general.

. . . In a way, love is all or nothing. You either express love or you don't. We can grow in our ability to be free and to understand ourselves, because these are skills to be learned and developed. But love is a gift of God. That's why when people first open up to the Spirit, open up to the love of God, it becomes hard for them to have uncharitable thoughts about other people or to harbor hatred in their hearts—because love and hatred have nothing in common. Darkness and light have nothing in common, and once love overtakes you, you simply can't sit around filled with hatred and bitterness anymore.

To be open to God's gift of love doesn't mean we're not tempted. Fleeting thoughts may come into us—impatience or dislike of another person—but we don't feed those thoughts and build on them. With love in our hearts, we find it hard to watch another person being torn down. And when we see love being violated, it does something in our guts. Love has taken over our lives, and there is no room for nonlove.

THE SCHOOL AND THE LESSON

There is a rhythm between hermitage and community that might be even more basic than the classic tension called action and contemplation. One is the school; the other is the lesson.

THE REIGN OF HEAVEN

The proclamation of the Reign of Heaven is the most radical political and theological statement that could ever be made. It has nothing to do with being perfect. . . . The Gospel is before all else a call to live differently, so that life can be shared with others. In other words, the Gospel is ultimately calling us to a stance of simplicity, vulnerability, dialogue, powerlessness, and humility. These are the only virtues that make communion and community and intimacy possible.

THE CENTER FOR ACTION AND CONTEMPLATION

The problems of the spirit can't be resolved with the brain. We have to move in the direction of a more body-related therapy and in the process give more weight to the right half of the brain. We also have to find forms of therapy more oriented to action. We named our center the Center for Action and Contemplation, deliberately putting action first. We learn and are healed by committing ourselves.

THE NEED FOR WISDOM IN ACTION

I've met so many people in the world who are already full of love and who really care for others. I believe that what we lack isn't love but wisdom. It became clear to me that I should pray above all else for wisdom in the decade to come.

We all want to love, but as a rule we don't know how to love rightly. How should we love so that life will really come from our love? . . . We haven't helped people to enter upon the narrow and dangerous path of true wisdom. On this path we take the risk of making mistakes. On this path we take the risk of being wrong. That's how wisdom is gained. On the spiritual path the enemy isn't pain; it's fear of pain. We haven't become wise, because we're so afraid of pain.

I believe that there are two necessary paths enabling us to move toward wisdom: a radical journey inward and a radical journey outward. For far too long we've confined people to a sort of security zone, a safe midpoint. We've called them neither to a radical path inward, in other words, to contemplation, nor to a radical journey outward, that is, to commitment on the social issues of our time.

We prefer to stay in a secure middle position, probably because these two great teachers, the inner and the outer way, both cause pain. Failure and falling short are the best teachers; success has practically nothing to teach on the spiritual path. But we notice that many of us incline to the one side or the other, on account of either temperament or education. Wherever I travel in the Church, I find people who focus inward and people who are activists. These two types seldom come together, and thus they both miss half the Gospel, they both lack half the truth.

I feel certain that we in the West have to begin primarily with action. The great temptation of the Western Church has been to imprison the Gospel in our heads. Up there we can be right or wrong, our position can be correct or false, but in any case everything always remains firmly in our grip. On the other hand, action never allows us the illusion of control, at least not for long.

TAKE A STEP BACKWARD

In religious circles one often runs into ideologues: right-wingers, left-wingers, liberals, conservatives. They all supervise life from an imaginary control tower in their head. Sometimes that grows wearisome. So long as we all cling to our prejudices and identify with our preconceived views and feelings, genuine human community is impossible. You have to get to the point where you can break free from your feelings. Otherwise in the end you won't have any feelings; they'll have you. Sometimes, however, one meets people who are free from themselves. They express what moves them— and then they can, so to speak, take a step backward. They play an active part in things, but you notice that they don't think they've got a corner on the truth market. Without this kind of "inner work," which consists in my simultaneously putting myself forward and relativizing myself, community is doomed to failure.

How many church communities and political action groups come to grief because of the incapacity of church authorities and parish councils to deal with one another in this way? Learning this is really hard work. This is far more than an entertaining parlor game. I probably can't expect it from politicians, but I do expect it from people who know God. It's the work of detachment, self-emptying, and "fasting"—the disciplines taught by all great world religions.

A NEW WAY OF LIVING

Some Christian groups have tried to do things differently. First it was the monks, hermits, and anchorites—moving out of, away from, and against the demands of empire—and "anchoring" themselves to something and Someone more substantial. Then it became the various religious orders and movements, some within the Mother Church, some without. But the common theme was a recognition that first you had to withdraw before you could engage effectively. You had to detach in order to attach, you had to deny before you could accept, you must empty out before Incarnation is possible. In very concrete and specific ways—such as dress, economics, authority, ownership, sexuality, draft exemption, simplicity of life, mobility, accountability, and so on—Christian groups pulled apart from the dominant consciousness to exemplify a new way of living.

In Catholic circles, these lifestyles tended to take celibate form and lumped these values together in the name of "poverty, chastity, and obedience." In Protestant settings, Christians tended to move into radical lifestyle groupings like the Waldensians, Hutterites, Quakers, Shakers, Mennonites, and Amish. This was attractive to Catholic reformers like St. Dominic, who told his friars, "Believe like the Catholics, but live like the Protestants." But in both of these cases, we see the consistent Christian recognition that there must be some kind of free choosing against the flow of culture.

PROTECTED INTERIORITY

Protected interiority was the historic meaning of cloister, vows of silence, silence in church, and guarded places and times inside of monasteries, where you were relieved of all the usual social pleasantries and obligations. Some had to be free to move beyond ego consciousness to deeper contact with the unconscious, the shadow self, the intimate journey of the soul, toward conscious union with God. Traditionally, you were never allowed to live as a "hermit" until later in life, and only after you had paid your dues to community and concrete relationships. Only community and marriage force you to face, own, and exorcise your own demons. Otherwise, loners are just misanthropes or sociopaths, people with poor social skills, or people who desire to have total control of

their day and time. This is not holiness. Avoiding people does not compute into love of God; being quiet and alone does not make you into a contemplative. Introversion and shyness are not the same as inner peace or communion. "Still waters run deep," they say, but that water can be either very clear or quite toxic.

ANNOUNCING THE ALTERNATIVE

We North Americans really don't know how to live in peace or without enemies. Our economy, our self-image, our very psyche have lived in a triumphalist and paranoid stance for so long that it will be hard to change to a positive and creative mode. But what can we do except continue to live and to announce the alternative: a new way of living based on faith instead of fear, peacemaking instead of moneymaking, community instead of competition. We are so addicted to the latter that it is hard to imagine the former. But Jesus is our imagination, and he told us that resurrection would come!

RADICAL HELP

After decades of counseling, pastoring, and clumsy attempts at helping other people, I am coming to a not so obvious but compelling conclusion: Much of our helping is like hoping for first-class accommodations on the *Titanic*. It feels good at the moment but it is going nowhere. The big tear in the hull is not addressed, and we are surprised when people drown, complain, or resort to lifeboats. Most of the people I have tried to fix still need fixing. The situation changed, but the core was never touched.

But what is the core? And how do we touch it? What does it mean essentially to help another person? If we can find the answer to these questions, we are coming close to what the world religions mean by true ministry. It is absolutely unlike any other form of helping. It has many counterfeits and disguises. What Jesus, Buddha, Confucius, the saints, and the prophets are talking about is the Absolute Help, which alone is worthy of the name—the radical help that none of us can give to another. We can only point to it and promise that it is there. That is the first and final work of all true religion. All else is secondary.

Call it grace, enlightenment, peak experience, baptism in the Spirit, revelation, consciousness, growth, or surrender, but until such a threshold is passed, people are never helped in any true, lasting sense. After the early stages of identity and belonging are worked through, real transformation does not seem to take place apart from some kind of contact with the Transcendent or Absolute. We now live in a secular culture that is largely afraid to talk about such contact except in either fundamentalist or vague New Age language. Neither is sufficient to name the depth or the personal demand of the true God encounter. What characterizes the trustworthy conversion experience is a profound sense of meeting Another, who names me personally and yet calls me to a task beyond

127

myself. Therapeutic healing will always be an effect, but it is never the goal itself or even a concern. One's own wholeness pales into insignificance in relationship to the Wholeness one is now delighting in.

CALLING OTHERS TO HEAL

Holiness has always been a very difficult concept to describe or define. People usually settle for an image of sweetness, soft piety, churchiness, humility, or asceticism. But I believe holiness can only be recognized by its effect in others. No one can claim it for himself or herself, as if it were a possession. Holiness is just that quality in a person which calls others to healing, forgiveness, conversion, and liberation from the self.

TRUSTING THE MASCULINE SOUL

A masculine spirituality would be one that encourages men to take that radical Gospel journey from their unique beginning point, in their own unique style, with their own unique goals—without doubt or apology or imitation of their sisters (or mothers, for that matter). That of itself takes

immense courage and self-possession. A man with such a spirituality has life for others and knows it. He does not need to push, intimidate, or play the power games common to other men, because he possesses his power with surety and calm self-confidence. He is not opinionated or arrogant, but he knows. He is not needy or bothered by status symbols, because he is. He does not need monogrammed briefcases and underwear, his identity is settled and secure—and within. He possesses his soul and does not give it lightly to corporations, armies, nation-states, and the acceptable collective thinking.

Saints trust their masculine soul because they have met the Father. He [*sic*] taught them about anger, passion, power, and clarity. He told them to go all the way through and pay the price for it (don't send the bill to others). He shared with them his own creative seed, his own decisive Word, his own illuminating Spirit. They are comfortable knowing and they are comfortable not knowing. They can care and not care without guilt. They can act without success because they have named their fear of failure. They do not need to affirm or deny, judge or ignore. But they are free to do all of them with impunity. The saints are invincible. They are men!

FRANCIS OF ASSISI: WARRIOR FOR LOVE

My Father, Francis of Assisi, said simply and well, "I am the Herald of the Great King." Francis never stopped being a warrior-knight. He just found a greater king. His image of self and victory changed. His goals grew broader, his heart deeper. He was still ready to spill blood for the cause, but now it led him to a personal visit to the Sultan in Egypt in the very midst of the bloody Christian Crusades.

He was prepared to offer his male milk, his blood, not for the violent death of any enemy but for the nonviolent victory of love.

Warrior energy needs to be wholly dedicated and given somewhere or to something, whether the somewhere or something is worthy or true. It must be focused and released for the warrior to know that she or he is alive and has character. Both in Iraq and in America the goals are seen as unimportant; it's just important that the warriors stand for something or someone. Our work, however, is to find worthy causes and goals to receive worthy warrior energy.

SPIRITUALITY REQUIRES ACCOUNTABILITY

Right now, contemplation is "in" within many religious and even secular circles. It is a way of being spiritual without any usual accountability, social action, or quality control. It is a way to be religious without being part of a religion. No dues, no priesthood, no commandments, no social grouping, no I-Thou relationship if you don't care for one. It utterly appeals to the Western individualist and introvert, and the ego payoff is major—a very superior self-image: "I am a mediator. I live in serenity above the fray of religious scandals and social concern." There is no system of checks and balance unless I allow it, and no God except the one I experience and decide for. I can do it all in the privacy of my own home and attend conferences and workshops that I judge to be worthy. The small self risks being utterly enthroned. There are no outer reference points of Scripture, society, or symbol to call me out of myself and back to Reality. And remember, "Reality is the best ally of God."

APOCALYPTIC PROPHETS: THE ABSOLUTE STANCE

The apocalyptic prophet has two simultaneous and self-correcting messages: (I) Everything matters immensely, and (2) it doesn't really matter at all. How many people do you know who can live out their lives on that pure and "narrow path"? I don't know very many. It seems that some are called to take the strongly apocalyptic position and all of the accompanying criticism in order to free the rest of us from our overengagement with and idolatry of "the way things are." Probably the most visible and effective witnesses to this position in our time are Dorothy Day and her "holy anarchy" and Thomas Merton's leaving it all to sit in a hermitage in the hills of Kentucky. They will always be open to criticism for not doing more, but their absolute stance, we have clearly seen, becomes the home and school for the emergence of true prophets.

Without the apocalyptic "No," prophets are no more than high-energy and idealistic activists, often working out of their own denied anger or denied self-interest. Apocalypticists are willing to be seen as fanatics, anti-American, anti-anything so that the rest of us can again discover the Absolute. They are bothered and bored by our relativities and rationalizations. They demand an objective Ground from which all else is judged and will not be nudged from their uncompromising stance. I believe one has to be a true and lasting contemplative to maintain the apocalyptic firmness and freedom.

RECONSTRUCTION

It is time for reconstruction. We need to know what we do believe, why we are proud of our-only-past, what is good about even the broken things (life, church, state), and how we can begin a new language of responsibility. At this point, I think anything else is a waste of time and refusal of grace. Human life is too short to waste it on the negative. It is too easy to be cynical.

I commit whatever years I have left to reconstruction (not regression or rigidity!) of a church and culture of meaning. Otherwise we will have no positive alternative ready when the deconstructed system falls apart. I have no doubt that it will, because love is always stronger than death.

GOOD OVER EVIL:
"THE BEGINNING IS ALWAYS HAPPENING"

Jesus believes that love will always rise from the dead, good is more powerful than evil, and his Father will prove this once and for all in his human body. Until we know that in our bones, until we risk it in our actions, until we base our life's choices on such awesome trust, "All our preaching is useless and all our believing is in vain" *(1 Cor. 15:14)*. The mystery of the death and resurrection of Christ tells us that it is finally a Benevolent Universe, God is on our side, we belong here, and there is no basis for existential fear. We no longer need to control, because something much better is already in the works. The Easter Mystery says that the true apocalyptic message is not "The end is near!" but "The beginning is always happening!" Power cannot see that. Love can see nothing else.

NOTES

Unless otherwise noted, all books copyright Richard Rohr and first published by The Crossroad Publishing Company.

Adam = *Adam's Return: The Five Promises of Male Initiation.* ©2004

Contemplation = *Contemplation in Action* ©2006

Enneagram = *The Enneagram: A Christian Perspective.* Richard Rohr and Andreas Ebert. Translated by Peter Heinegg. Original German edition published as *Das Enneagram: Die 9 Gesichter der Seele.* © Claudius Verlag, 1989. Revised and expanded German edition © Claudius Verlag, 1999. English translation of the first German edition published as *Discovering the Enneagram: An Ancient Tool for a New Spiritual Journey*, ©1990 by The Crossroad Publishing Company. This translation of the revised and expanded German edition ©2001 by The Crossroad Publishing Company.

Everything = *Everything Belongs: The Gift of Contemplative Prayer.* Revised and updated edition. ©1999, 2003

Grace = *Grace in Action*, by Richard Rohr, OFM, and Others. Edited by Teddy Carney and Christina Spahn. ©1994 Center for Action and Contemplation.

Job = *Job and the Mystery of Suffering.* ©1998

Luke = *The Good News According to Luke: Spiritual Reflections.* ©1997

Naked = *The Naked Now.* © 2009

Quest = *Quest for the Grail.* ©1994

Simplicity = *Simplicity: The Freedom of Letting Go.* Revised and Updated. Originally published as *Von der Freiheit loszulassen—Letting Go*, translated and introduced by Andreas Ebert. © Claudius Verlag Munich, 1990. English translation ©1991. Revised English language edition ©2003. Translated by Peter Heinegg.

Five: CONTEMPLATION MEANS PRACTICING HEAVEN HOW

PHOTO CREDITS

PAGE 56: Photograph of Thomas Merton's Hermitage by Paul M. Pearson. Used with per-mission. PAGE 57: Photograph of Thomas Merton by John Lyons. Used with permission of the Merton Legacy Trust and the Thomas Merton Center at Bellarmine University. PAGE 59: Stairway to forest c lkunl, Fotolia.com. PAGE 61: Carol M. Highsmith. PAGE 65: Зимняя сказка с Maria Moroz, Fotolia.com. PAGE 66: William Blake, "Job Rebuked by His Friends, from the Butts set. Pen and black ink, gray wash, and watercolor, over traces of graphite." Public Domain. PAGE 69: Leonardo da Vinci. PAGE 72: "Jonah and the Whale," folio from Jami al-Tavarikh (Compendium of Chronicles), circa. 1400, attributed to Iran. Public Domain. PAGE 74: Sunrise on a lake c Elena Petrova, Fotolia.com. PAGE 75: Albert Einstein. The Library of Congress. Public domain. Photograph by Oren Jack Turner, Princeton, N.J. PAGE 76: Therese von Lisieux, Adrian Michael. Source: Infotafel Augsburg. Public Domain. PAGE 78: Sailboats. Maria Schayer- Gorska. Public Domain. PAGE 80: Chen Hongshou [Public domain]. PAGE 82: Moses and bush, Eugene Pluchart. Public domain via Wikimedia Commons. PAGE 87: Drawing of the Crucifixion by St. John of the Cross circa 1550. Public Domain. PAGE 89: Vintage image of the Virgin Mary carrying baby Jesus c kmiragaya, Fotolia.com. PAGE 91: "The Last Judgment," Fra Angelico (circa 1395–1455), medium: tempera on wood. Museo di San Marco, Florence. Public Domain. PAGE 94: Martin Buber. The David B. Keidan Collection of Digital Images from the Central Zionist Archives (via Harvard University Library). Public Domain. PAGE 97: Eyes by anonymous. Public domain. PAGE 100: Eric Hoffer in bathrobe with pipe, writing at table, 1967. William Gedney Photographs and Writings, David M. Rubenstein Rare Book & Manuscript Library. http://library.duke.edu/digitalcollections/gedney. PAGE 102: Painting by unknown artist from Cusco in the 18th century. Public Domain. PAGE 105: Dorothy Day, Milwaukee Journal photo, courtesy of the Department of Special Collections and University Archives, Marquette University Libraries. PAGE 109: Ibn Arabi (1164–1240). Album/Art Resource, NY. page. PAGE 113: Die Sudkuppel im Esonaitliex dei Kariye cami in Istanbul. Public Domain. PAGE 116: New York World-Telegram and the Sun staff photographer: DeMarsico, Dick, photographer. [Public domain]. PAGE 118: The Arrest of Mahatma Gandhi in his house in 1932. Beltrame, Achille (1871–1945). Art Resource, NY. PAGE 120: Father with Downs Syndrome son c Monkey Business, Fotolia.com. PAGE 125: Das Wiedersehen (Meeting Again). [The group depicts Christ and the apostle, Thomas] 1926. Bronze. Barlach, Ernst (1870–1938). Munson-Williams-Proctor Arts Institute/Art Resource, NY. PAGE 127: Blackburn, Jemima, 1823-1909 [No restrictions]. PAGE 128: Saint George in stained glass c Howgill, Fotolia.com. PAGE 133: Isenheim Altarpiece, Matthias Grunewald. Public Domain.

You Might Also Like

THOMAS KEATING
THE HEART OF THE WORLD
An Introduction to Contemplative Christianity

Paperback, I00 pages, ISBN 978-0-8245-24951

The Christian heritage is rich in contemplative wisdom,
literature, and practices. As fresh and vibrant today as
when it was first published, this classic book is essential
to a deeper understanding of the spiritual center of
Christianity. It is especially written for those who,
while benefiting from a spiritual practice in one of the
other world religions, want to preserve or renew their
fundamental commitment to Christianity.

~ excerpts from this book on following two pages ~

Support your local bookstore
or order directly from the publisher at
www.CrossroadPublishing.com

To request a catalog or inquire about quantity orders,
please e-mail sales@CrossroadPublishing.com

The Crossroad Publishing Company

CHRISTIAN SPIRITUALITY

For the early Fathers of the Church there was only one spirituality, the spirituality of Jesus Christ, who died and rose again, and who is pouring out his Spirit over the world. As time went on, the richness of the mystery of Christ tended to be differentiated. Christ is too big a reality to be fully expressed by any one individual or any one vocation. Yet all expressions, all vocations, must be rooted in him.

The apostolic expression was powerful in the early Church and is especially strong again today as it works for world peace, justice, and service of the poor. On the other hand, there are always persons who are called by the Spirit to a greater participation in the mystery of Christ's silence and solitude through a life organized for the growth of contemplation. There is no opposition between action and contemplation. Rather, it is a question of emphasis and of one's aptitude and vocation from God. The institutional lifestyles that gradually evolved over the centuries have become known as the active and contemplative lives.

But there are further differentiations. Various religious movements have been raised up by the Spirit in the course of the centuries to meet certain needs of the time. Each movement has a special spirituality that goes back to the particular vision of its founder. But these particularities must not be emphasized to the detriment of the ultimate spirituality that belongs to every Christian. This ultimate reality is the indwelling Spirit who makes of us a temple of God, Father, Son and Holy Spirit. This one point needs to be strongly emphasized: every Christian, by virtue of the grace of baptism, has the vocation to oneness with the Father through Jesus Christ in the Holy Spirit.

Everyone needs some kind of practice in order to accomplish this vocation. Obviously, a rule of life cannot be as detailed for those living in the world as it is for people in a monastery. But everyone has to build his or her own kind of enclosure as far as one's duties allow, by setting aside a certain amount of time every day for prayer and spiritual reading. Also, perhaps, one may dedicate a day every month, and a week every year, to being alone with the Lord. Jesus himself encouraged this in the Gospel when he said to the apostles, "Come away by yourselves to a lonely place, and rest a while" (Mark 6:31).

It is difficult to establish a rule of life to which one

You Might Also Like

JOAN CHITTISTER
THE RULE OF BENEDICT
A Spirituality for the 21st Century

Paperback, 328 pages, ISBN 978-0-8245-25941

Today's major spiritual inquiries such as stewardship, relationships, authority, community, balance, work, simplicity, prayer, and psychological development are all addressed in this fifteen-hundred-year-old classic known as *The Rule of Benedict*. With extraordinary vision and common sense, this rule, written by Benedict of Nursia, the founder of Western monasticism, guides us into a new way seeing and living that can transform our modern world just as it did 1500 years ago.

The Crossroad edition presents the complete text of the Rule. It also offers practical and inspiring commentary for our lives today from Benedictine sister Joan Chittister, one of the most influential and spiritual leaders of our age.

"A prophetic voice that is desperately needed
in our troubled time."
—Karen Armstrong, author, *The Great Transformation*

~ excerpts from this book on following two pages ~

Support your local bookstore
or order directly from the publisher at
www.CrossroadPublishing.com

To request a catalog or inquire about quantity orders, please
e-mail **sales@CrossroadPublishing.com**

The Crossroad Publishing Company

THE RULE OF BENEDICT *Insights for the Ages*

INTRODUCTION

The Rule of Benedict, ancient as it is, has a very subtle power and a very serious problem, as well: it is extremely simple to read. There is nothing convoluted about it, nothing metaphysical. On the contrary. The Rule of Benedict is direct; it is clear; it is a relatively uncomplicated text that uses simple language to make simple references to simple things that have meaning even now after 1,500 years. As a result, it is difficult to miss what is being said in it. There is little wonder it has lasted so long. At the same time, because it is so unvarnished, so uncomplicated in its structure, so simple in its concepts, it is also fairly easy to discount its concern for early sixth-century agendas and fairly difficult to recognize its continuing value. It's an essentially straightforward, clean-spoken document, true, but not always very relevant, it seems, to twenty-first century culture and lifestyles. To readers who have inherited the mysticism of the Middle Ages, the treatises of the scholastic philosophers, and the theology texts of centuries of church life, it is almost incomprehensible that this brief document, almost 1,500-years old, is now enshrined as one of the greatest spiritual handbooks of all time. Volumes have been written about it but the small, unassuming text itself is almost bound to be disappointing to a culture that likes things to sound impressive and to look slick.

What is it, then, that the Rule of Benedict says to the sixth century that gives it not only the right but the need to be heard by the twenty-first century as well? What is it about the Rule of Benedict that stays both authentic and necessary century after century after century in culture after culture after culture?

The answer surely lies more in the ideas with which it concerns itself and the attitudes it sets out to form than in the particulars it prescribed for the people who were reading it in early Europe.

The Rule of Benedict is not concerned with a single time and place, a single view of church, a single set of devotions or a single ministry. The Rule of Benedict is concerned with life: what it's about, what it demands, how to live it. And it has not failed a single generation.

The Prologue to the rule is its cornerstone and its gauntlet. Read this, the rule says, and if this is not what you're about, do not read on.

A Complete List of
Richard Rohr's Crossroad Titles

THE NAKED NOW.
LEARNING TO SEE AS THE MYSTICS SEE

QUEST FOR THE GRAIL

CONTEMPLATION IN ACTION

SIMPLICITY. THE FREEDOM OF LETTING GO

ADAM'S RETURN.
THE FIVE PROMISES OF MALE INITIATION

EVERYTHING BELONGS.
THE GIFT OF CONTEMPLATIVE PRAYER

THE GOOD NEWS ACCORDING TO LUKE.
SPIRITUAL REFLECTIONS

THE ENNEAGRAM. A CHRISTIAN PERSPECTIVE

JOB AND THE MYSTERY OF SUFFERING.
SPIRITUAL REFLECTIONS

GRACE IN ACTION

ABOUT THE AUTHOR

Fr. Richard Rohr, O.F.M., is a globally recognized ecumenical teacher bearing witness to the universal awakening within Christian mysticism and the Perennial Tradition. He is a Franciscan priest of the New Mexico Province and founder of the Center for Action and Contemplation (CAC) in Albuquerque, New Mexico. Fr. Richard's teaching is grounded in the Franciscan alternative orthodoxy—practices of contemplation and lived kenosis (self-emptying), expressing itself in radical compassion, particularly for the socially marginalized.

Fr. Richard is the author of numerous books, including *The Naked Now, Everything Belongs, Adam's Return, Breathing under Water, Falling Upward, Immortal Diamond*, and *Eager to Love: The Alternative Way of Francis of Assisi*.

Fr. Richard is academic Dean of the Living School for Action and Contemplation. Drawing upon Christianity's place within the Perennial Tradition, the mission of the Living School is to produce compassionate and powerfully learned individuals who will work for positive change in the world based on awareness of our common union with God and all beings.

Fr. Rohr has been a featured essayist on NPR's *This I Believe*, a guest of Dr. Mehmet Oz on the *Oprah and Friends* radio show, and has been interviewed by Oprah Winfrey on the Oprah Winfrey Network's show, *Super Soul Sunday*. He also appears in the documentary *ONE*, that features spiritual teachers from around the world.

ABOUT THE EDITOR

John Norman Jones, PhD (1964–2012), served as the Editorial Director of The Crossroad Publishing Company for over twelve years. Jones did much to help shape the direction of Crossroad and Herder & Herder by building long-term relationships with both established authors and new voices. He worked on important books by writers such as Meister Eckhart, Bernard McGinn, Richard Rohr, Henri Nouwen, Timothy Gallagher, Ronald Rolheiser, George Weigel, Gregory Popcak, Rowan Greer, Paula D'Arcy, and others.

He helped to develop the manuscripts of first-time authors with extraordinary skill and empathy, though he rarely accepted credit for the role he played in the finished book. Instead, his focus was on the work—the way it might energize the theological debates of the day and bring the reader further along in the search for truth. Like a true mystic, he held his own life lightly even as he took it seriously. He owned little, and he spent long hours in meditation. Though an accomplished poet and scholar in his own right, he chose instead to work as an editor, placing his considerable gifts in service to the thought and writing of others.

About the Publisher

The Crossroad Publishing Company publishes Crossroad and Herder & Herder books. We offer a 200-year global family tradition of books on spiritual living and religious thought. We promote reading as a time-tested discipline for focus and understanding. We help authors shape, clarify, write, and effectively promote their ideas. We select, edit, and distribute books. Our expertise and passion is to provide wholesome spiritual nourishment for heart, mind, and soul through the written word.